PC SCHEME MiniManual
to accompany Appleby & VandeKopple:
Programming Languages:
Paradigm and Practice

PC SCHEME MiniManual

To accompany Appleby & VandeKopple:
Programming Languages: Paradigm and Practice
Second Edition

Richard G. Hull

Lenoir-Rhyne College

THE McGRAW-HILL COMPANIES, INC.

New York   St. Louis   San Francisco   Auckland   Bogotá   Caracas
Lisbon   London   Madrid   Mexico City   Milan   Montreal   New Delhi
San Juan   Singapore   Sydney   Tokyo   Toronto

McGraw-Hill

*A Division of The **McGraw·Hill** Companies*

PC SCHEME MINIMANUAL
to accompany Appleby & VandeKopple:
Programming Languages: Paradigm and Practice

1 2 3 4 5 6 7 8 9 0 BKM BKM 9 0 9 8 7 6

ISBN 0-07-005317-0

This book was set in Palatino by Cecelia G. Morales.
The editor was Eric M. Munson.
The production supervisor was Diane Ficarra.
The design manager was Charles A. Carson.
Project supervision was done by Cecelia G. Morales.
Book-mart Press, Inc., was printer and binder.

http://www.mhcollege.com

CONTENTS

PREFACE

The second edition of this MiniManual coincides with the publication of *Programming Languages: Paradigm and Practice,* Second Edition, by Doris Appleby and Julius VandeKopple (McGraw-Hill, 1997). This MiniManual was designed as part of a series of minimanuals to accompany the Appleby and VandeKopple text. Through these manuals, students in a programming languages course can gain actual hands-on experience with a variety of today's languages and programming paradigms.

In the world of functional programming, LISP and its descendants hold a prominent place, and it is with this position in mind that a manual for a LISP-like language should be among those available. There were many languages to choose from, having a wide range of complexity and cost, from the public-domain XLISP to the more complex Common LISP. SCHEME was chosen because it is a small, clean dialect of LISP with many nice features, and, with the advent of PC SCHEME from Texas Instruments, it became an inexpensive choice. (See the section "Changes in the Second Edition" for more information about PC SCHEME versions and availability.)

With this text, I have attempted to provide a brief introduction to programming in PC SCHEME. The emphasis is on functional programming techniques, and the early chapters concentrate on a functional subset of the language. Later chapters present alternative approaches, such as imperative and object-oriented programming. In selecting material I have tried to include several explicit examples, both long and short, of the various programming techniques discussed, and many concepts are first introduced in these examples. Such examples help to motivate the inclusion of various language features as well as to illustrate their use in actual programming situations that are manageable by beginning SCHEME programmers. For a more complete discussion of the advanced SCHEME features mentioned in Chapter 12, the reader is directed to one of the many fine full-size textbooks currently on the market, and listed in the references.

This manual can be used in its entirety in conjunction with the *Programming Languages* text. Laboratory exercises provided with that text build upon the ideas and examples presented in this manual. Students should have access to the full set of PC SCHEME manuals from Texas Instruments and to the PC SCHEME system itself.

This manual may also be used independently as a text for a short course in SCHEME. It is recommended that one take the chapters in the order presented, since many examples are continued from chapter to chapter. Chapter 10 may be omitted if necessary, with no loss of continuity. Chapter 11 as well may be omitted, though it contains examples of several useful programming techniques that are part of the standard SCHEME repertoire. (In fact, an effort was made to present a variety of techniques, perhaps even at the expense of some efficiency and consistency.)

CHANGES IN THE SECOND EDITION

Since the publication of the first edition of this MiniManual, there have been a number of developments in the SCHEME world. As the popularity of the language has grown, several additional implementations have become available at little or no cost. PC SCHEME has been sold by Texas Instruments to Ibuki, who plans to develop it further. The last version available from Texas Instruments, version 3.03, is available free over the Internet via anonymous ftp from altdorf.ai.mit.edu in the directory /archive/pc-scheme/. This version conforms to the Revised[3] Report. Several other SCHEME implementations are also available by anonymous ftp from altdorf.ai.mit.edu and from the SCHEME Repository at nexus.yorku.ca, many conforming to the Revised[4] Report, which was released in 1991. A notable commercial version is EdScheme, from Schemers, Inc., with versions for DOS and Macintosh systems. Both Ibuki and Schemers, Inc., have promised future Windows-compatible versions.

In this edition, I have moved the PC SCHEME-specific chapters on editing and debugging to Appendixes C and D, added some material on lazy evaluation using `delay` and `force`, and corrected one or two errors that somehow crept into the earlier version. New code was run using PC SCHEME version 3.03, obtained from altdorf.ai.mit.edu as described above, running under Windows 3.1. Code was again pasted into the text, this time using Word for Windows 2.0c, and I continue to believe that all examples should run correctly as printed, in particular the corrected definition of `define-macro` in Appendix B.

Richard G. Hull

CHAPTER 1

A First, Informal Session with SCHEME

SCHEME, like its parent language LISP, is an interactive language. But unlike the popular interactive versions of the *imperative* language BASIC, SCHEME is primarily a *functional* language. When we sit at the computer terminal to interact with SCHEME, we will not be giving imperative instructions to be executed, but rather we will be asking SCHEME for the value of various expressions. The form of these expressions make up the syntax of the SCHEME language and will be described in more detail in the following chapters. For now, we shall begin by focusing on simple arithmetic expressions.

1.1
STARTING A PC SCHEME SESSION

We invoke PC SCHEME at the DOS prompt by entering one of the following:

pcs	For the standard memory version (640K)
pcsexp	For the expanded (LIM) memory version
pcsext	For the extended memory version

We are first greeted with an opening message giving the version number and date, the memory version selected (no message for standard version), and a copyright notice. This is followed by the information:

```
[PCS-DEBUG-MODE is OFF]
```

and the first prompt. (More will be said about PCS-DEBUG-MODE later.) The PC SCHEME prompt is of the form [n], where n is the number of the next expression to be entered. That is, the interpreter, or "Listener," keeps track of how many expressions it has evaluated and shows you the next number in its prompt.

1

1.2
ENDING A PC SCHEME SESSION

Before going much further, we should also mention how to leave the PC SCHEME environment. At the prompt, simply type (exit) and press [RETURN] (or [ENTER]).

    [1] (exit)

(exit) is an example of a SCHEME function. Unlike most other SCHEME functions, as described below, it does not return a value; before it can return anything, the session comes to an end and we are returned to DOS. (Ending the session is a side effect of evaluating the exit function. In functional programming, side effects are generally to be avoided, but a few such as this will remain with us.)

1.3
ARITHMETIC EXPRESSIONS

The prompt indicates that the SCHEME Listener is ready to evaluate an expression. The simplest arithmetic expressions are individual numbers, which evaluate to themselves, as follows:

    [1] 3
    3
    [2] 3.25
    3.25
    [3] -5
    -5
    [4] _

We may also ask for the value of various operations on numbers, such as addition, multiplication, etc. Expressions involving operators are written in parenthesized prefix notation: (<operator> <argument1> <argument2> ...); for example,

    [4] (+ 2 5)
    7
    [5] (* 2 5)
    10
    [6] (abs -5)
    5
    [7] (sqrt 5)
    2.23606797749979
    [8] (sqrt -5)

    [ERROR encountered!] Invalid argument to SQRT
    -5

    [Inspect] Quit
    [9] _

Notice that when we try to evaluate (sqrt -5), we generate an error. In PC SCHEME this puts us into a new environment called the "Inspector." For now, we will simply return to the "top-level" prompt by pressing CTRL-Q (for Quit).

```
[9] (sin 1.3)
0.963558185417193
[10] (+ 1 2 3 4)
10
[11] (= 2 2)
#T
[12] (= 2 3)
()
[13] _
```

In [10] we see that + can take more than two arguments. (In fact, it can take any number of arguments, as can the * function.) The values returned by expressions [11] and [12] represent TRUE and FALSE, respectively. We will discuss these values subsequently.

In addition, we may compose operators in fully parenthesized expressions, as follows:

```
[13] (+ 2 (* 3 4))
14
[14] (* (+ 1 2) (* 3 4))
36
[15] (= 3 (+ 1 2))
#T
[16] (sqrt (* 3 4))
3.46410161513776
[17] (* (sqrt 5) (sqrt 5))
5.
[18] (sqrt (* 5 5))
5.
[19] _
```

This notation, with its many parentheses, may seem difficult at first, but it becomes more comfortable with practice. What may come as a surprise is that with these few examples you have seen essentially all there is to see about the syntax of SCHEME. All SCHEME programming consists of defining and evaluating such expressions. All that remains is to investigate the additional built-in operators and functions and how to define our own functions.

The function compositions above are possible because all SCHEME functions use *call-by-value* for parameter passing. Some "special forms" violate this rule, but for the most part any functions which we define will use call-by-value only. Thus when we evaluate an expression like (+ (* 3 4) (* 2 5)), before + is applied, the values of the arguments (* 3 4) and (* 2 5) are computed, and the *values* are passed to +. If we use only call-by-value functions, we should have no problems with unwanted side effects. However, we will find that some side effecting (recall (exit)) is present and in fact desirable in SCHEME. Without side effects, we would have no traditional I/O.

1.4
SYMBOLS

LISP and SCHEME are often described as *symbol-processing* languages. In mathematics, we first replaced numbers with symbols in algebra. While these symbols are used to represent numbers, we perform many operations on them which require something more than arithmetic. For example, the formula $(a + b)^2 = a^2 + 2ab + b^2$ can certainly be used with numbers substituted for a and b, but it is more valuable when used as is or with variables or algebraic expressions (involving variables) substituted. Such manipulations of symbols can be quite tedious in many familiar languages. However, symbol manipulations are at the heart of LISP and SCHEME, hence their wide use in programs dealing with symbolic mathematics and natural languages.

Given the above, one might ask if we can use letters in place of numbers in SCHEME expressions to be evaluated. The answer can be guessed if we first ask what the value of $x + 3$ would be in algebra. We can only say, "It depends upon the value of x." Such is also the case with SCHEME. The expression (+ x 3) cannot be evaluated unless x itself has a value. If we try to evaluate (+ x 3), an error is generated, and we again enter the Inspector environment.

```
[1] (+ x 3)

[VM ERROR encountered!] Variable not defined in current environment
X

[Inspect] Quit
[2] _
```

The symbol x apparently has no default value here in what is called the "top-level environment" of SCHEME. In fact, most symbols have no predetermined value. The few that do fall into two categories: (1) names of built-in functions, and (2) special symbols. We have encountered some built-in functions already:

```
[2] exit
#<PROCEDURE EXIT>
[3] +
#<PROCEDURE +>
[4] *
#<PROCEDURE *>
[5] _
```

The evaluator responds with the information that these symbols have values which are built-in procedures. (In later chapters, we will discuss further the very important idea that SCHEME procedures can be treated as values to be manipulated and returned.) We also find that the following special symbols have predetermined values.

```
[5] t
#T
[6] true
#T
[7] #t
#T
```

```
[8] false
()
[9] nil
()
[10] #f
()
[11] _
```

SCHEME provides a recognizer function for objects of the symbol type, called symbol?. However, if we try to apply it as follows, we get a familiar error.

```
[11] (symbol? x)

[VM ERROR encountered!] Variable not defined in current environment
X


[Inspect] Quit
[12] _
```

What has happened is that the SCHEME evaluator has tried to evaluate the argument to the function symbol? and failed. So how, you might ask, can we demonstrate this function? One way would be to give it an argument that evaluates to a symbol. As we shall soon see, there are several of these. For now, however, let us consider the following *special form,* quote. The form quote takes one argument and, unlike regular functions, returns its argument unevaluated.

```
[12] (quote x)
X
[13] (quote (+ 2 3))
(+ 2 3)
[14] _
```

quote is used so often that the system provides us with a short form. The expression 'x is automatically expanded to (quote x) by the SCHEME Listener. The above can thus be simplified to:

```
[12] 'x
X
[13] '5
5
[14] '(+ 2 3)
(+ 2 3)
[15] _
```

And now we can try symbol?:

```
[15] (symbol? 'x)
#T
[16] (symbol? 5)
()
[17] (symbol? '5)
()
[18] _
```

1.5
LISTS

The expression quoted in [14] above is called a *list* in SCHEME. As we shall see, lists play an important part in SCHEME programming. Evaluation of lists is described in Chapter 2. But treating them simply as data objects, we can apply several SCHEME functions. Note that quoting a list prevents evaluation of the elements of the list.

```
[18] (symbol? '(1 2 3))
()
[19] (length '(a b c d e))
5
[20] (reverse '(a b c d e))
(E D C B A)
[21] _
```

The empty list is represented by (). It is recognized by the function null?.

```
[21] '()
()
[22] (length '())
0
[23] (null? '())
#T
[24] (null? '(a b c))
()
[25] _
```

The function list takes an arbitrary number of arguments and returns a list of those arguments.

```
[25] (list 1 2 'a 4 '(3 b))
(1 2 A 4 (3 B))
[26] _
```

1.6
COMMENTS

A semicolon (;) is used in SCHEME to indicate a comment. The comment begins with the semicolon and continues to the end of the line. Thus a multiline comment must begin with a semicolon on each line, for example,

```
[27] (+ 2 5 3 4)   ;+ may take many arguments
14
[28] ;in fact, + can take any nonnegative number
     ; of arguments, including 0 or 1
(+ 3)
3
[29] (+)
0
[30] _
```

CHAPTER 2

A Closer Look at SCHEME Data

In Chapter 1, we restricted most of our examples to numeric data. LISP and SCHEME, however, are better known for their ability to process symbolic data. The arithmetic expressions of Chapter 1 are special cases of "symbolic expressions" or simply "expressions." Expressions consist primarily of atoms and lists.

2.1
ATOMS

The basic data objects of SCHEME are *atoms*, of which there are three types: numbers, strings, and symbols.

Numbers

   Examples: 2, -5, 1.03, 2.5e-3

Numbers evaluate to themselves. Thus, if you enter a number such as 2 at the SCHEME prompt, the system will respond with a 2, which is the value of your expression. What you would see is:

```
[1] 2
2
[2] _
```

   Numbers can represent integer or floating point values. Integers are of arbitrary precision, dependent upon the amount of memory available to store the digits. (This dependency is due to the fact that integers are in fact processed symbolically as lists of digits, rather than as equivalent binary values, as in most other languages.)

Strings

Strings—sequences of characters enclosed in quotes (")—also evaluate to themselves, for example:

```
[2] "hello"
"hello"
[3] "34"
"34"  ◄———— Note this is the string containing the two characters
[4] _             "3" and "4", and not the number 34.
```

Symbols

Examples: `foo, x, this-is-a-long-symbol-name, 785n4%!#`

Most symbols do not have a predefined value. Thus, if you try to evaluate them, you will generate an error. There are, however, a few important symbols that do have predefined values, as we saw in Chapter 1. They are used to represent TRUE and FALSE, and are the following:

Constants: `#T` prints as `#T`
              `#F` prints as `()`

To provide compatibility with earlier versions of SCHEME, the constants `#!TRUE` and `#!FALSE` are also provided, but `#T` and `#F` should be used for any new code written.

Variables: `true` initially has the value `#T`
              `false` initially has the value `#F`

Note: Variables in SCHEME are much like those in other languages. They are used to hold values and are said to be *bound* to those values. The set of all variables and associated values in effect at any time is called the current *environment*. Variables such as `true` and `false` can be given different values by methods that will be presented later.

To provide compatibility with other LISP dialects, SCHEME also provides the atoms `t` and `nil`. When the environment variable `PCS-INTEGRATE-T-AND-NIL` is set to `#T` (the default situation), `t` and `nil` are identified with `#T` and `#F` respectively. When `PCS-INTEGRATE-T-AND-NIL` is `#F`, `t` and `nil` become variables like `true` and `false`.

2.2
LISTS

Perhaps the most important data structure of LISP, and thus of SCHEME, is the *list*. A list is a sequence of expressions enclosed in a set of parentheses. The expressions within the list may be atoms or lists themselves. Some SCHEME lists are:

```
(1 2 3)                          (a b c d e)
(1 2 (3 d a) ((5)) a (1 (1)))    (x)
(+ 2 (- 3 4))                    (car a)
()
```

While a list may be treated simply as a data object, we know also that the list (+ 2 (- 3 4)) can be evaluated as a functional form. The SCHEME evaluator handles lists as follows:

1. The first element of the list is evaluated and must evaluate to a *function.*
2. The rest of the elements of the list are evaluated and their values are passed as *arguments* to the function which was the *value* of the first element.
3. The result of applying the function (1) to the arguments (2) is returned as the value of the list.

SCHEME also contains some special forms which may appear in the function position of a list, but which receive some or all of their arguments unevaluated. Among these are quote, which returns its argument unevaluated, and define, which will be discussed further in Chapter 3.

An attempt to evaluate a list such as (1 2 3) would result in the following:

```
[1] (1 2 3)
[ERROR encountered!] Attempt to call a nonprocedural object
(1 2 3)
[Inspect] Quit
[2] _
```

The empty list () can in fact be evaluated without error, and evaluates to itself.

```
[2] ()
()
[3] _
```

(Compare this with the evaluation of ' () as in Chapter 1.)

2.3
PAIRS

The fundamental underlying data structure of SCHEME is the *pair.* It corresponds to an ordered pair of SCHEME objects. The pair whose first element points to the atom A and second to the atom B is denoted by (A . B) and is often diagrammed as shown in Figure 2.1.

Pairs cannot generally be evaluated, and are used primarily to build complex data structures. Many texts and many programmers get along quite well without ever dealing with pairs explicitly.

One data structure in particular that is built using pairs is the SCHEME list as described in the previous section. Those familiar with linked lists as implemented in

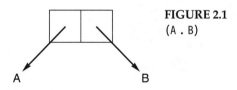

FIGURE 2.1
(A . B)

Pascal, C, etc., will see that the pairs correspond nicely to records, where one field is (the pointer to) an item in the list, and the other field is a pointer to the rest of the list. The SCHEME list (A B C) is represented by the pair structure (A . (B . (C . NIL))), as illustrated in Figure 2.2.

In SCHEME, all the pointers necessary to build such lists are built-in and hidden from the programmer. There is no need to do explicit storage allocation and deallocation, as space is allocated as needed at run time, and reclaimed by automatic "garbage collection" also at run time.

Pairs are constructed by the SCHEME function cons, that is:

```
[1] (cons 'a 'b)
(A . B)
[2] (cons 'a nil)    ; (A . NIL)
(A)
[3] _
```

Note that while [1] produces a pair, [2] produces a list with the one element, A, as shown in Figure 2.3. The list (A B C) can be constructed as follows:

```
[3] (cons 'a (cons 'b (cons 'c nil)))
(A B C)
[4] _
```

For reasons dating back to the first implementation of the LISP language, the functions that select the two components of a pair are called car and cdr. car returns the first element of a pair and cdr returns the second.

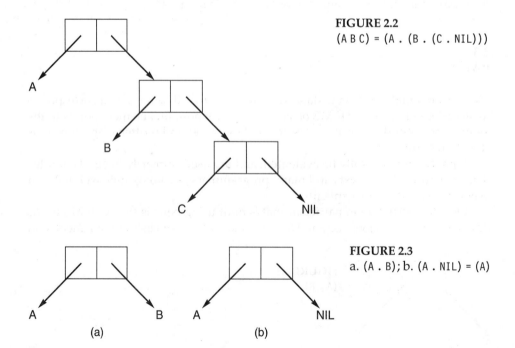

FIGURE 2.2
(A B C) = (A . (B . (C . NIL)))

FIGURE 2.3
a. (A . B); b. (A . NIL) = (A)

(a)   (b)

```
[4] (car '(a . b))
A
[5] (cdr '(a . b))
B
[6] _
```

Combinations of these functions, such as:

```
[6] (car (cdr '(a . (b . c))))
B
[7] _
```

can be abbreviated by:

```
[7] (cadr '(a . (b . c)))
B
[8] _
```

Such abbreviations can be used up to (cxxxxr *<expr>*), where each x may be replaced by either an a or a d, with the expected meaning, e.g., (caddr x) = (car (cdr (cdr x))).

Since lists are represented by pair constructs, we can apply car and cdr to them. Note that the car of a list returns the first element, and the cdr returns the rest of the list.

```
[9] (car '(a b c))
A
[10] (cdr '(a b c))
(B C)
[11] _
```

Similarly, cons can be used to add a new element to the front of an existing list.

```
[11] (cons 'a '(b c d))
(A B C D)
[12] _
```

The relationship between car, cdr, and cons is given by the following equations:

```
(cons (car L) (cdr L)) = L
(car (cons x L)) = x
(cdr (cons x L)) = L
```

2.4
TESTING EQUALITY OF SCHEME OBJECTS

Atoms are so named because they are indivisible data objects, while pairs and lists are composite or structured objects. This difference is important when we consider equality tests. The predefined SCHEME function eq? tests its two arguments to see if they are identical, i.e., bound to the same actual memory location. If those arguments are symbols, eq? will return #T if they are equal and () if not. However, if the arguments are structured, eq? will not test for structural equality. Two different pairs with the same components will test unequal with eq?. The SCHEME function equal?

performs the deeper test of structure for use on pairs and lists. Finally, a third function, eqv?, tests equality of two atoms—including numbers and strings, as well as symbols.

```
[1] (eq? 'x 'x)
#T
[2] (eq? 'x 'y)
()
[3] (eq? "hello" "hello")
()
[4] (eqv? "hello" "hello")
#T
[5] (eq? '(a b c) '(a b c))
()
[6] (eqv? '(a b c) '(a b c))
()
[7] (equal? '(a b c) '(a b c))
#T
[8] (equal? '(a b) '(b a))
()
[9] (equal? '(a b (c d) e) '(a b c d e))
()
[10] (equal? '(a b (c d) e) '(a b (c d) e))
#T
[11] _
```

Numbers provide some interesting results:

```
[11] (eq? 5 5)
#T
[12] (eq? 500000 500000)
()
[13] (eqv? 500000 500000)
#T
[14] (equal? 500000 500000)
#T
[15] _
```

SCHEME has the power to deal with arbitrary-precision integer values. It gets this power by treating large numbers as lists of numeric symbols. Thus, small numbers may be stored in a single memory location and eq? comparisons will work, but larger numbers are structured, causing eq? to fail.

2.5
RECOGNIZERS

The various SCHEME data objects can be recognized by the predefined functions symbol?, number?, string?, and pair?. The function atom? recognizes all atomic SCHEME objects, including numbers, symbols, and strings. There is no separate predefined recognizer for lists, since they are implemented as pairs. Some authors, in fact, call data objects such as (a . (b . c))—which would print in SCHEME as (A B . C)—"dotted lists." However, such "lists" must be treated differently from true lists when defining functions, and throughout this text we will never refer to such dotted lists as lists, in order to distinguish between them clearly.

2.6
A STYLE NOTE

The functions car and cdr extract the components of a pair. As such, they also may be applied to lists, and in fact, such application is important in SCHEME. But the names are far from mnemonic (unless you know their ancient history), and they do little to enhance program readability. Newer versions of LISP, notably Common LISP, have introduced the functions first and rest to deal with lists. These new functions are, in fact, equivalent to car and cdr respectively, but much more readable. By using the SCHEME special form define, we may add these functions to our programs as follows:

```
[1] (define first car)
FIRST
[2] (define rest cdr)
REST
[3] _
```

We may then rewrite one of our previous examples as:

```
[3] (first '(a b c))
A
[4] (rest '(a b c))
(B C)
[5] _
```

We may also define:

```
[6] (define second cadr)
SECOND
[7] (define third caddr)
THIRD
[8] (define fourth cadddr)
FOURTH
[9] _
```

yielding results such as:

```
[9] (third '(a b c d e))
C
[10] _
```

PC SCHEME provides a way for us to add such patches to the SCHEME system through the use of certain files that are evaluated as the system is loaded. Each of these files is read in and all of the expressions contained in them are evaluated in the top-level SCHEME environment. Two of these files are listed below, in the order that they are loaded.

patch.pcs   Located in the SCHEME home directory or a directory in the defined DOS path—used for modifications to the general SCHEME system

scheme.ini   Located in the current directory—used for modifications specific to particular applications

If we place the following in patch.pcs in our SCHEME directory, we will have the use of the above-mentioned functions whenever we load SCHEME.

```
(define first car)
(define second cadr)
(define third caddr)
(define fourth cadddr)
(define rest cdr)
```

This file can be created using any text editor, including the SCHEME editor EDWIN, which is described in Appendix A.

From this point on in this text, we shall use first, rest, etc., for lists and reserve car and cdr for pairs.

CHAPTER 3

Defining Your Own Functions

We have seen in Chapter 1 how we can evaluate functions that are fairly complex combinations of the predefined SCHEME functions. Consider, for example, the function:

$$f(x) = x^2 + 2x + 3$$

To evaluate $f(5)$ in SCHEME, we would enter:

```
(+ (* 5 5) (* 2 5) 3)
```

To evaluate $f(\sin(1.3))$, we would need:

```
(+ (* (sin 1.3) (sin 1.3)) (* 2 (sin 1.3)) 3)
```

This function requires evaluating (sin 1.3) three times. If SCHEME were an imperative language, we might try:

```
(assign x (sin 1.3))      ; x := sin(1.3)
(+ (* x x) (* 2 x) 3)
```

But the purely functional subset of SCHEME (to which we have attempted to restrict ourselves) contains no assignment statement. However, let us look again at the given function.

$$f(x) = x^2 + 2x + 3$$

We might write:

$$f(5) = (5)^2 + 2(5) + 3$$

or:

$$f(\sin(1.3)) = (\sin(1.3))^2 + 2(\sin(1.3)) + 3$$

In each of these functions, the left side contains only one reference to the argument. We could improve on our SCHEME version if we could represent the function f itself by a SCHEME expression and then apply it to whatever argument we choose.

3.1
LAMBDA EXPRESSIONS

We can use a notation derived from Church's lambda calculus to represent the function f as:

$$f = \lambda x \, . \, x^2 + 2x + 3$$

In SCHEME, this lambda expression can be written as:

```
(lambda (x) (+ (* x x) (* 2 x) 3))
```

allowing us to do the following:

```
[5] ((lambda (x) (+ (* x x) (* 2 x) 3)) 5)
38
[6] ((lambda (x) (+ (* x x) (* 2 x) 3)) (sin 1.3))
5.85556074751886
[7] _
```

This is still quite clumsy, though. We need a way to associate the lambda expression with a function *name* such as f. We make this association by using the special form define, as follows:

```
[1] (define f
      (lambda (x) (+ (* x x) (* 2 x) 3)))
F
[2] _
```

define officially returns an unspecified value (although many implementations return the function name, in this case, f) and has the side effect of associating the lambda expression:

```
(lambda (x) (+ (* x x) (* 2 x) 3))
```

with the symbol f. This side effect allows the following simple function call:

```
[2] (f 5)
38
[3] (f (sin 1.3))
5.85556074751886
[4] _
```

When (f 5) is evaluated, the lambda variable x is bound to the value of the actual argument 5, and then the expression (+ (* x x) (* 2 x) 3) is evaluated in an extended environment in which x is defined and has the value of the argument. Note that x is still undefined at the top level.

SCHEME also allows a simplified version of define that eliminates the explicit reference to lambda:

```
[1] (define (f x)
      (+ (* x x) (* 2 x) 3))
F
[2] _
```

The effect of this version of define is identical to that of the first.

3.2
EXAMPLES

```
[1] (define (sqr x) (* x x))
SQR
[2] (define (discriminant a b c)
      (- (sqr b) (* 4 a c)))
DISCRIMINANT
[3] (define (absolute-value x)
      (if (negative? x)
        (- x)
        x))
ABSOLUTE-VALUE
[4] _
```

Example [3] introduces another special form of SCHEME. The if function provides a conditional expression corresponding to the if...then...else... type construct of imperative languages. The general form is:

```
(if <test-expr>
  <expr-1>
  {<expr-2>})
```

If <test-expr> evaluates to true—anything other than #F or ()—then the value of <expr-1> is returned as the value of the if expression. Otherwise, the value of <expr-2> is returned. The expression <expr-2> is optional, and if it is omitted and <test-expr> evaluates false, the value of the if expression is unspecified in SCHEME. PC SCHEME actually returns (), however, and NIL is returned in many LISP dialects.

Using the list and dotted-pair functions mentioned in Chapter 2, we can define new functions such as:

```
[4] (define (fifth l)
      (car (cddddr l)))
FIFTH
[5] (define (reverse-pair dtpr)
      (cons (cdr dtpr) (car dtpr)))
REVERSE-PAIR
[6] (define (make-singleton-list x)
      (cons x nil))
MAKE-SINGLETON-LIST
[7] _
```

In order to expand our repertoire we must look further into SCHEME's control structures. This is the subject of Chapter 4.

3.3
FUNCTIONS ACCEPTING AN ARBITRARY
NUMBER OF ARGUMENTS

SCHEME also provides a feature that is hard to come by in Pascal-like languages—user-defined functions that can take a variable number of arguments. Pascal does provide built-in procedures such as read and write, which have this property, but the programmer can define only procedures and functions that take a fixed number of arguments. SCHEME also provides built-in procedures of this type; we have already seen +, *, and list, for example. In fact, we actually can define three types of functions: (1) those with a fixed number of arguments, (2) those with a completely arbitrary number of arguments, and (3) those with a fixed number of required arguments and an additional arbitrary number of optional arguments. We have already dealt with type (1) above, so let us next look at type (2).

Recall that there are two forms of define that we can use to define a function:

1. (define foo (lambda (x y) ...))
2. (define (foo x y) ...)

In order to have foo take an arbitrary number of arguments, we would modify the first of these to read:

1. (define foo (lambda x ...))

Note that rather than providing a list of the formal parameters, we have used an atom as the only formal parameter. When this function is called, the *atom* x will be bound to a *list* of the actual arguments in the call. Note, for example, that (lambda x x) is a function that returns a list of its actual arguments—i.e., it is the previously seen SCHEME function list. The second form above requires a dotted-pair notation for the formal parameter, as follows:

2. (define (foo . x) ...)

Most functions of this type require some conditional processing of the formal parameter to deal with the unknown number of actual arguments, and thus are beyond our capabilities at this point. We will return to this topic in Chapter 6. For now, a fairly simple example might be the following function, which takes an arbitrary number of arguments and returns a list of those arguments in reverse order. Notice that it can be called with as few as zero arguments.

```
[1] (define (rev-list . lst)
      (reverse lst))
REV-LIST
[2] (rev-list 3 4 5 6 7)
(7 6 5 4 3)
[3] (rev-list 2 3)
```

```
(3 2)
[4] (rev-list 3)
(3)
[5] (rev-list)
()
[6] _
```

Finally, we can define functions of type (3) described above, which take some required and some optional arguments. The defining forms are combinations of the forms for types (1) and (2), as one might expect. They are exemplified by:

1. `(define foo (lambda (x y . z) ...))`
2. `(define (foo x y . z) ...)`

Each of the above forms would define a function, `foo`, which takes two required arguments, passed to the formal parameters x and y, and arbitrarily many additional arguments, a list of which would be passed to the formal parameter z. The following function returns the value of its first argument incremented by its second argument, if a second argument is present, and incremented by 1 if not.

```
(define (inc x . amount)
  (if (null? amount)
    (+ x 1)                        ; or equivalently (1+ x)
    (+ x (first amount)))))
```

3.4
USING CONDITIONAL EXPRESSIONS

As a final note, consider the following rewrite of `inc` which takes advantage of the fact that the `if` form provides SCHEME with ALGOL-like conditional expressions.

```
(define (inc x . amount)
  (+ x (if (null? amount) 1 (first amount)))))
```

While this is more concise, avoiding the repetition of the (+ x ...) call, we might question its relative readability. At times, such a construct may be natural, but in this case I think most of us, and most LISP/SCHEME programmers I've known, would opt for the original definition.

CHAPTER 4

A Closer Look at SCHEME Control

The traditional control concepts of sequencing, selection (branching), and repetition (looping) find fairly direct translation into the more familiar imperative languages. These concepts can also be handled by SCHEME, but in a slightly different form. Program control in LISP and SCHEME often causes initial problems for those whose background has been limited to imperative languages, and thus deserves some careful study. In this chapter, we take a look at control in SCHEME from a functional point of view and compare it to imperative programming in Pascal-like languages. Repetition in SCHEME is pursued further in Chapter 6, with examples more closely attuned to true SCHEME programming style. Finally, in Chapter 9, we shall consider additional control structures of SCHEME, which are more imperative in nature.

4.1
SEQUENCING

In an imperative language, *sequencing* refers to executing a sequence of commands in a given order. But in pure functional languages, we do not have *commands*. Instead, we have only function application. What then might we mean by sequencing?

As an illustration of sequencing, consider the SCHEME interpreter ("Listener") itself. Each time an expression is entered, the following sequence of actions must take place:

1. Read the expression (from the keyboard or a file).
2. Evaluate the expression.
3. Write the resulting value on the screen.

In a language like Pascal, we have built-in procedures for reading and writing. As for evaluation, we might implement this step with a procedure, evaluate(e,v), which assigns v the value of the expression e. Our sequence might then be written as:

```
begin
      read(e);
      evaluate(e,v);
      writeln(v)
end
```

We might also implement evaluation as a function, evaluate(e), which returns the value of e. We would then write:

```
begin
      read(e);
      v := evaluate(e);
      writeln(v)
end
```

But we could also combine the second and third steps, giving us:

```
begin
      read(e);
      writeln(evaluate(e))
end
```

If read were also a function, returning the value read from the appropriate input device, we could write the entire sequence as a single function composition, as follows:

```
begin
      writeln(evaluate(read))
end
```

The equivalent SCHEME function call is:

```
(writeln (eval (read)))
```

For more information on the functions read and writeln, as well as other input/ output functions, see Chapters 5 and 8. The function eval is built into SCHEME and performs the desired evaluation. eval evaluates (the value of) its argument. Its availability to the SCHEME programmer, along with the fact that SCHEME programs and SCHEME data have the same form, allows us to define functions that build lists representing SCHEME code and then execute that code—a very powerful feature of the language.

As another example of SCHEME sequencing, consider the following algorithm to add an element to the tail end of a list (sometimes called "snoc" in LISP circles since it does the reverse of cons).

1. Reverse the list.
2. Add the item to the front of this reversed list.
3. Reverse the result of step 2.

A programmer familiar only with the imperative style might try the following (assuming the existence of an "assign" function):

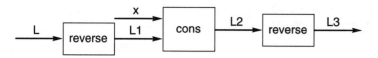

FIGURE 4.1
Function composition chain for `add-to-rear`

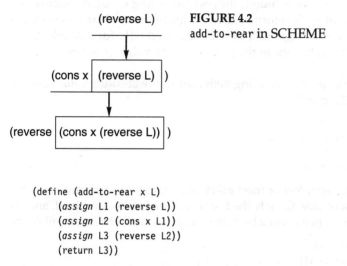

FIGURE 4.2
`add-to-rear` in SCHEME

```
(define (add-to-rear x L)
    (assign L1 (reverse L))
    (assign L2 (cons x L1))
    (assign L3 (reverse L2))
    (return L3))
```

A functional approach to the problem is illustrated in Figure 4.1. Each function is represented by a box, which takes in certain input values and emits a result. Reading the diagram from left to right we see the above sequence of events.

We capture the left-to-right flow in Figure 4.1 by building our final function from the inside, as illustrated in Figure 4.2, and written in SCHEME as:

```
(define (add-to-rear x L)
    (reverse (cons x (reverse L))))
```

Notice that the result of computing (reverse L) is sent as the second argument to the cons call, and the result of the cons is sent to the outer reverse. The sequence of calculations starts with the innermost reverse and ends with the outermost reverse.

4.2
SELECTION

Selection, or branching, is handled through the use of conditional expressions. Conditional expressions have been around for quite some time, from their early appearance in LISP and ALGOL, to current languages such as C. A conditional expression is one that may return alternative values depending upon the (Boolean) value of some condition(s). The traditional LISP conditional expression is formed with the cond (short for "conditional") operator. The syntax is shown on the next page.

```
(cond (<p₁>, <e₁,₁>, <e₁,₂> ... <e₁,ₖ₁>)
      (<p₂>, <e₂,₁>, <e₂,₂> ... <e₂,ₖ₂>)
                        .
                        .
                        .
      (<pₙ>, <eₙ,₁>, <eₙ,₂> ... <eₙ,ₖₙ>))
```

Semantically, the p_i are evaluated, one at a time, until one returns a true (non-null) value. When such a true value is found, the corresponding e_{ij} are evaluated, one at a time, and the value of $e_{i,ki}$ is returned as the value of the cond expression. Since the values of the earlier e_{ij} are ignored, they can be used only for side effect. (Examples will follow shortly.) If none of the p_i are true, the value of the expression is unspecified.

As an example, consider the following definition of the absolute value function introduced earlier in Chapter 3.

```
(define (absolute-value x)
   (cond ((negative? x) (- x))
         ((zero? x)     0)
         ((positive? x) x) ))
```

Of course, this is not the simplest or most efficient way to define this function, but it demonstrates the use of cond. Clearly the last two cases can be combined, and the final test is unnecessary, since it must be true at that point. A refinement might be:

```
(define (absolute-value x)
   (cond ((negative? x) (- x))
         (#T            x) ))
```

In this version, the last test predicate is #T, which evaluates to itself, and thus is non-null. If the first case is not taken, the second certainly will be. It is the LISP equivalent of an else clause, and SCHEME has taken this one step further by allowing the keyword else to be used in this case.

```
(define (absolute-value x)
   (cond ((negative? x) (- x))
         (else          x) ))
```

Note that else is a syntactic keyword, which provides the equivalent of a true expression in the last case of a cond. It does not have a value at top level.

Of all these definitions, the simplest may still be the one from Chapter 3, using the if form:

```
(define (absolute-value x)
   (if (negative? x)
       (- x)
       x ))
```

But before we discard cond we should note that it is generally the more straightforward way to write multiway branches such as:

```
(cond ((positive? discriminant)
        (find-two-real-solutions ...))
      ((zero? discriminant)
        (find-one-real-solution ...))
      (else
        (find-complex-solutions ...)))
```

An important note about the evaluation sequence in the cond and if expressions is that tests and expressions are evaluated only when needed (lazy evaluation). Thus, we may have functions such as:

```
(define (foo x)
  (if (negative? x)
      0
      (sqrt x)))
```

In function foo, (sqrt x) will be evaluated only when the test (negative? x) has evaluated to false. Similarly, we may have:

```
(define (bar x)
  (cond ((negative? x) 1)
        ((< (sqrt x) 10) 2)
        (else 3) ))
```

In function bar, the second test, (< (sqrt x) 10), will be evaluated only if (negative? x) has tested false.

4.3
REPETITION

Since sequencing is handled by function composition, it seems only natural that repetition, which involves a sequence that repeats itself, should be handled by function composition that repeats itself in some way. When the result of a function evaluation is used in the construction of one or more arguments to another call to that same function, we have *recursion*. In purely functional subsets of LISP or SCHEME, all repetition is implemented by recursion.

Perhaps the simplest type of repetition would be an infinite loop—repetition that never ends. The LISP/SCHEME Listener discussed at the beginning of this chapter is an example of such a loop; to terminate it, you must end the LISP/SCHEME session. The algorithm for this loop is:

```
loop
      read an expression
      evaluate the expression
      write the value
end loop
```

As mentioned previously, the body of this loop is a simple sequence of operations that can be written in SCHEME as:

```
(writeln (eval (read)))
```

The following definition would execute this body once:

```
(define (lisp)
  (writeln (eval (read))))
```

In order to repeat, we must finish with another call to the main function. However, the following contains a syntax error:

```
(define (lisp)
  (lisp (writeln (eval (read)))))
```

Did you spot the error? The call to lisp involves passing it one argument—the body of the loop—but the definition is for a parameterless function. This situation can be remedied by using a helper function as follows:

```
(define (lisp)
  (lisp-loop #T))

(define (lisp-loop x)
  (lisp (writeln (eval (read)))))
```

The argument passed to lisp-loop in the definition of lisp can be any defined value. #F would work just as well, as would any integer, for example. We may also use an optional parameter, as in:

```
(define (lisp . x)
  (lisp (print (eval (read)))))
```

The loop is terminated when the expression (exit) is read and evaluated.

4.4
BOUNDED LOOPS

It is probably more common to use finite rather than infinite loops. Since SCHEME is primarily a list-processing language, the simplest and most natural examples come from looking at lists of symbols. One of the predefined list functions mentioned in Chapter 2 was length. Had it not been provided, we could have designed and implemented such a function, call it list-length, using the following (recursive) algorithm:

> if the list is empty then
> > return a length of 0
>
> else
> > return a value 1 greater than the length of the "rest" of the list (i.e., all but the first element)

In SCHEME, this algorithm becomes:

```
(define (list-length 1)
  (if (null? 1)
    0
    (add1 (list-length (rest 1)))))
```

Note the use of rest rather than cdr for readability. Recall that rest is not predefined and must be provided by the user, as described in Chapter 2.

As another example, we may at times find it convenient to have a (side-effecting) function that prints all the elements of a list in some desired form, and which may be defined in terms of a user-defined write-element function.

```
(define (write-list 1)
  (cond ((null? 1)
          *the-non-printing-object*)
        (else
          (write-element (first 1))
          (write-list (rest 1)))))
```

Recall that this is a function and as such returns a value. In the first cond alternative, it returns *the-non-printing-object*, a value that does not appear on the screen, while in the else alternative it returns whatever is returned by the recursive call—eventually that same nonprinting object. We would assume that this function will only be called for its side effect and not for the value returned.

SCHEME offers a shortcut to a similar result. The predefined function for-each takes two arguments, the first of which evaluates to a function and the second of which is a list. SCHEME then applies the function to each of the elements of the list in succession and finally returns #T. Thus we could redefine write-list as:

```
(define (write-list 1)
  (for-each write-element 1))
```

At the SCHEME top level, write-list will return (and display on the screen) the value returned by for-each, i.e., #T. However, when write-list is used inside another function in a place where the returned value is ignored, this return should cause no problems.

4.5
ADDITIONAL LOOPING EXAMPLES

Additional examples of recursively defined list functions will be considered in Chapter 5. The following looping examples are presented for comparison with perhaps more familiar imperative languages, such as Pascal, and to further demonstrate SCHEME programming techniques. They are not necessarily representative of common SCHEME programming style.

While Loops

The decision to terminate a loop may be based upon a test made at the beginning
of each pass, as in the Pascal **while** loop. Consider the following Pascal example,
which prints a column of integers starting with 1 and ending with the largest integer whose square is smaller than some given number max.

```
n := 1;
while ( sqr(n) < max ) do
    begin
        writeln(n);
        n := n + 1
    end;
```

The SCHEME version of this Pascal example involves defining two functions, one
to control the loop (here called print-loop) and one to initialize the control values
n and limiting-value (here called print-numbers).

```
(define (print-loop n max)
  (cond ((> (sqr n) max)
            *the-non-printing-object*)
          (else
            (writeln n)
            (print-loop (add1 n) max))))

(define (print-numbers max)
  (print-loop 1 max))
```

The SCHEME procedure writeln is very similar to the Pascal procedure of the same
name. It writes the value of its argument on the screen, followed by a carriage return. One remaining detail is to define the sqr function, which is not predefined in
SCHEME:

```
(define (sqr n) (* n n))
```

A comment is in order: print-numbers does its work by side effect. Its purpose
is to print numbers on the screen. Thus we can use the sequence of expressions in
the else clause. A more purely functional approach might be to define a function
that returns a list of the desired numbers:

```
(define (list-numbers max)
  (list-loop 1 max '()))

(define (list-loop n max number-list)
  (if (> (sqr n) max)
      (reverse number-list)
      (list-loop (add1 n)
                 max
                 (cons n number-list))))
```

If we then desired to print the list as above, we would use a function like write-
list as previously defined (replacing write-element by writeln):

```
(define (print-numbers max)
  (write-list (list-numbers max)))
```

Loops with Counters

Next we will consider loops that are executed a given number of times, based on values determined at the beginning of each loop's execution. For a simple example, consider a loop to print the integers from 1 to a given value n in a single column on the screen. In Pascal, this might be accomplished by:

```
for i := 1 to n do
    writeln(i);
```

This is equivalent to the following Pascal **while** loop:

```
i := 1;
while i <= n do
    begin
        writeln(i);   ·
        i := i + 1
    end;
```

Thus, in SCHEME we would again define two functions, one to control the loop and one to initialize the control values i and n.

```
(define (print-loop i n)
  (cond ((> i n)
            *the-non-printing-object*)
        (else
          (writeln i)
          (print-loop (add1 i) n))))

(define (print-to-n n)
  (print-loop 1 n))
```

These examples are a bit contrived, and certainly do not convince one to switch from Pascal to SCHEME. SCHEME's power is exhibited best in its symbolic list manipulations, as described more fully in Chapter 5. Loops such as the above are encountered infrequently. For those times when such loops are required, SCHEME provides iterative control structures, which are described in Chapter 9.

Two Sample Programs

5.1
EXAMPLE 1—SOLVING QUADRATIC EQUATIONS

For our first example of program development, let us consider the fairly simple problem of finding the real solutions to equations of the form:

$$ax^2 + bx + c = 0$$

where a, b, and c can be any real values.

The first step in solving such a problem is to determine the form of the expected input and output. Since the input will most likely be the three real numbers a, b, and c, we might expect to have a SCHEME function, `solve-equation`, which takes these real numbers as its three arguments, that is:

```
(define (solve-equation a b c) ... )
```

For output we can expect zero, one, or two real solutions. A suggestion might be to return a list of the real solutions, which can then be examined to determine the number of solutions, for example.

Given this situation, we begin to flesh out the definition of `solve-equation`. If the value of a is zero, we have at best a simple linear equation. Otherwise, we have a true quadratic. Using a top-down approach, we now begin to define `solve-equation`:

```
(define (solve-equation a b c)
  (if (zero? a)
      (solve-linear-equation b c)
      (solve-quadratic-equation ...)))
```

Before we get to the details of `solve-quadratic-equation`, let us define `solve-linear-equation`, which solves the equation $ax + b = 0$.

```
(define (solve-linear-equation a b)
  (if (zero? a)
    '()
    (list (/ (- b) a))))
```

Note that rather than use the parameters b and c, which match the actual arguments, we have chosen to define this function on its own, using the more common parameters a and b. The function is pretty straightforward. If a is zero, we do not have an equation in x, so an empty solution list is returned. Otherwise, we return the result of dividing -b by a.

Now let us look at solve-quadratic-equation. We might expect the parameters to be a, b, and c, in which case the function would look like:

```
(define (solve-quadratic-equation a b c)
  (cond ((zero? (- (* b b) (* 4 a c)))
          (find-one-solution a b))
        ((positive? (- (* b b) (* 4 a c)))
          (find-two-solutions a b c))
        (else
          '() )))
```

where:

```
(define (find-one-solution a b)
  (list (/ (- b) (* 2 a))))
```

and:

```
(define (find-two-solutions a b c)
  (list
    (/ (+ (- b) (sqrt (- (* b b) (* 4 a c))))
       (* 2 a))
    (/ (- (- b) (sqrt (- (* b b) (* 4 a c))))
       (* 2 a))))
```

But this function has a slight deficiency in that we must evaluate the discriminant (- (* b b) (* 4 a c)) a total of four times. What we need is a local variable—we would like to evaluate the discriminant once and assign the result to this local variable for future reference. However, we do not have assignment in the familiar sense. But we do have local variables—the formal parameters—and they are "assigned" values when we call the function with those values as the actual arguments. So, perhaps we can calculate the discriminant once and pass its value as an argument to solve-quadratic-equation. Note that we can then eliminate c as a parameter, since it is only used within the discriminant calculation.

```
(define (solve-quadratic-equation a b discrim)
  (cond ((zero? discrim)
          (find-one-solution a b))
        ((positive? discrim)
          (find-two-solutions ...))
        (else
          '() )))
```

We note further that `find-two-solutions` must calculate the square root of the discriminant twice—another chance for this type of improvement. To carry this approach to extremes for the purposes of this example, we can also avoid double calculation of (- b) and (* 2 a) by using the following definitions:

```
(define (find-two-solutions two-a minus-b discr-root)
   (list
       (/ (+ minus-b discr-root) two-a)
       (/ (- minus-b discr-root) two-a)))

(define (solve-quadratic-equation a b discrim)
   (cond ((zero? discrim)
           (find-one-solution a b))
         ((positive? discrim)
           (find-two-solutions
             (* 2 a) (- b) (sqrt discrim)))
         (else
           '() )))
```

All that remains is to call `solve-quadratic-equation` properly in our original `solve-equation` function, as follows:

```
(define (solve-equation a b c)
   (if (zero? a)
       (solve-linear-equation b c)
       (solve-quadratic-equation
               a b (discriminant a b c) )))
```

where:

```
(define (discriminant a b c)
   (- (* b b) (* 4 a c)))
```

Using `let`

A more readable alternative to the above technique also eliminates the extra evaluations, while still avoiding a side-effecting assignment operator. The special form `let` allows us to introduce a new environment with local variables bound to the values of given expressions. The basic form of `let` is:

```
(let ((<var> <form>) ... ) <expr> ... )
```

`let` extends the current environment to include the *<var>*s, bound to the values of the corresponding *<form>*s, and then evaluates the sequence of *<expr>*s within that extended environment. The value of the last of the *<expr>*s is returned. Thus we can write our previous definitions as follows:

```
(define (solve-equation a b c)
   (if (zero? a)
       (solve-linear-equation b c)
       (solve-quadratic-equation a b c) ))
```

```
(define (solve-quadratic-equation a b c)
  (let ((discrim (discriminant a b c)))
    (cond ((zero? discrim)
           (find-one-solution a b))
          ((positive? discrim)
           (find-two-solutions a b discrim))
          (else
           '() ))))
```

```
(define (find-two-solutions a b discrim)
  (let ((two-a (* 2 a))
        (minus-b (- b))
        (discr-root (sqrt discrim)))
    (list
      (/ (+ minus-b discr-root) two-a)
      (/ (- minus-b discr-root) two-a))))
```

The functions solve-linear-equation, find-one-solution, and discriminant need not be changed.

In the function solve-quadratic-equation, we introduced a new environment with only one local variable, discrim, which was initialized to the value of (discriminant a b c). However, in find-two-solutions, we have three local variables. Each of the *<form>*s must be evaluated and the values must be assigned to the variables. A question that arises is the order in which all these scenarios take place. In fact, there are two parts to this question: (1) in what order are the forms evaluated, and (2) is each assignment done immediately as the form is evaluated, or are all forms evaluated before any assignments? Since we may conceivably want to refer to one local variable in the initializing form for another, such as in:

```
(let ((discrim (discriminant a b c))
      (discrim-root (sqrt discrim))) ...)
```

the answers are important. And the answer is that SCHEME provides different forms to provide the various evaluation orders. For the form let, the *<form>*s are evaluated in the current environment (in an undetermined order) and all *<form>*s are evaluated before any assignments take place. Thus the let form immediately above would not work correctly. To provide sequential evaluation and assignment as we need here, SCHEME provides the form let*, which evaluates the first of the $<form_i>$ in the current environment and assigns its value to the first $<var_i>$. The second $<form_i>$ is then evaluated in the extended environment (including the first $<var_i>$ and its binding) and its value is assigned to the second $<var_i>$, and so on for each variable. Thus in:

```
(let* ((discrim (discriminant a b c))
       (discrim-root (sqrt discrim))) ...)
```

the form (sqrt discrim) is evaluated in an extended environment in which discrim is defined and has been bound to the value of (discriminant a b c).

A third form, letrec, introduces all of the $<var_i>$ into the extended environment before evaluating the $<form_i>$ (in an undetermined order), thus allowing recursive references.

Polishing Up the Output—Simple I/O

The following SCHEME transcript shows how our equation-solving functions might be used:

```
[1] (solve-equation 1 2 -3)
(1. -3.)
[2] (solve-equation 1 2 1)
(-1)
[3] (solve-equation 0 1 3)
(-3)
[4] (solve-equation 1 1 1)
()
[5] _
```

Floating point values are returned in [1] due to the use of sqrt in the quadratic equation. In [2] and [3], we were able to return integers (division of two integers returns an integer when possible).

From a functional programming point of view, it is acceptable and in fact quite desirable to return the list of solutions, which could then be passed to other related functions. Often, though, we may want to define a top-level driver for our program to provide input prompts and commented output, or to hide the implementation details from the user.

In order to provide more complex input/output, we must introduce a new set of SCHEME procedures. Any program's input/output involves side-effecting the outside world of screens, printers, disk drives, etc. Thus the SCHEME I/O procedures are not purely functional. Of the several I/O procedures in SCHEME, we will concentrate on three for now. Each procedure is defined to return an unspecified value. (As usual, when an implementation returns a value that is described as unspecified in the language description, that value should not be used in programs, since it may vary from one implementation to another.) The I/O procedures we will look at here are:

(display *<exp>*)	Prints the value of *<exp>* in a form designed for people to read
(newline)	Outputs a carriage return—like Pascal's *writeln* with no arguments
(writeln *<exp>*)	Prints the value of *<exp>* using display followed by a newline

It should be mentioned that SCHEME does have procedures called write and print, which output the value of their arguments in a form designed to be read in by a SCHEME program. We will discuss write and print further in Chapter 8.

Armed with these new procedures, we first write a procedure to print the list of solutions returned by solve-equation. Note the use of sequences of expressions in the three cond clauses, as mentioned in the previous chapter. In each case, the values of all but the last expression are lost, but we had no interest in their values anyway—we were interested in their I/O side effects.

```
(define (print-solutions L)
  (cond ((null? L)
         (newline)
         (writeln "No real solutions.")
         (newline)
         *the-non-printing-object*)
        ((null? (rest L))
         (newline)
         (display "The only real solution is x = ")
         (writeln (first L))
         (newline)
         *the-non-printing-object*)
        (else
         (newline)
         (writeln "The real solutions are:")
         (newline)
         (display "    x = ")
         (writeln (first L))
         (display "    x = ")
         (writeln (second L))
         (newline)
         *the-non-printing-object*)))
```

Sample run:

```
[5] (print-solutions (solve-equation 1 2 -3))

The real solutions are:

    x = 1.
    x = -3.

[6] (print-solutions (solve-equation 1 2 1))

The only real solution is x = -1

[7] (print-solutions (solve-equation 1 1 1))

No real solutions.

[8] _
```

The above calls are tedious enough to suggest that we write a new top-level function that combines the solving and the printing.

```
(define (solve a b c)
  (print-solutions (solve-equation a b c)))
```

Now we can do the following:

```
[8] (solve 1 2 -3)

The real solutions are:

    x = 1.
    x = -3.
```

```
[30] (solve 1 2 1)

The only real solution is x = -1

[31] (solve 1 1 1)

No real solutions.

[32] _
```

5.2
EXAMPLE 2—RIPPLE-CARRY ADDER

This next example is a bit more involved, both in background knowledge assumed and in SCHEME techniques used. We will begin with a description of the basic problem to be solved.

In this example, we will simulate the electronic components of a binary adder. We will then use this simulated adder to perform binary addition in SCHEME. Our binary adder will manipulate only the symbols 0 and 1, represented in SCHEME by the expressions |0| and |1|. Note that |0| is a *symbol*, which has the print-name 0, and is not the *number* 0. We will build up our adder using the basic logic gates defined in Table 5.1 and diagrammed in Figure 5.1.

Using these gates, we can build up our adder in steps. The first step is to build a "half-adder," which takes as input 2 bits and returns their sum, in the form of a one-digit sum and a carry; e.g., 1 + 1 yields a sum of 0 and a carry of 1, since in binary, 1 + 1 = 10. The structure of the half-adder is shown in Figure 5.2.

We now use two half-adders and an OR-gate to build a "full-adder," which incorporates a third input bit representing a carry-in to the operation. Its structure is shown in Figure 5.3. The final step is to link a number of full-adders together to

TABLE 5.1
Definitions of basic logic gates

a	b	a AND b	a OR b	a XOR b
1	1	1	1	0
1	0	0	1	1
0	1	0	1	1
0	0	0	0	0

FIGURE 5.1
Diagrams of basic logic gates

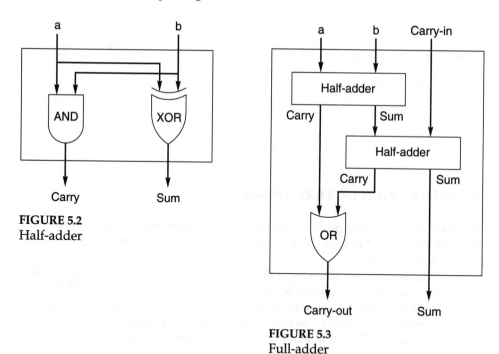

FIGURE 5.2
Half-adder

FIGURE 5.3
Full-adder

form a ripple-carry adder, as shown in Figure 5.4. While a true hardware implementation would contain a fixed number of full-adders, to handle binary numbers of a fixed (maximum) number of bits, we will be somewhat more lenient here and allow an arbitrary number of full-adders. Thus we will be able to use our simulation to add binary numbers of arbitrary length.

To build the SCHEME code for this simulation, we could use either a top-down or bottom-up approach. Having used a top-down approach in the previous example, let us do this one from the bottom up. Thus we first implement the logic gates. Recall that individual bits will be represented as the symbols |0| and |1|, not the integers 0 and 1.

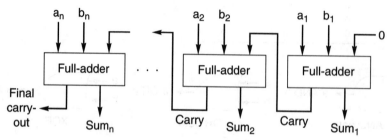

FIGURE 5.4
Ripple-carry adder: $b_n \ldots b_2 b_1 + a_n \ldots a_2 a_1$

```
(define (and-gate a b)
  (if (and (eq? a '|1|) (eq? b '|1|))
    '|1|
    '|0|))

(define (or-gate a b)
  (if (or (eq? a '|1|) (eq? b '|1|))
    '|1|
    '|0|))

(define (xor-gate a b)
  (if (and
        (or (eq? a '|1|) (eq? b '|1|))
        (not (and (eq? a '|1|) (eq? b '|1|))))
    '|1|
    '|0|))
```

To implement the half-adder, we will define two functions, one to return the sum and one to return the carry. (An alternative would be to define one function that returns a list of these two values, but then we would need to select the components of that list.)

```
(define (half-adder-sum a b)
  (xor-gate a b))

(define (half-adder-carry a b)
  (and-gate a b))
```

The full-adder is handled in a similar way:

```
(define (full-adder-sum a b carry-in)
  (half-adder-sum
    (half-adder-sum a b)
    carry-in))

(define (full-adder-carry a b carry-in)
  (or-gate
    (half-adder-carry a b)
    (half-adder-carry (half-adder-sum a b) carry-in)))
```

Finally, we come to the full ripple-carry adder. At this point, we must decide the format of the adder's input and output. We are not yet concerned with top-level user I/O, but rather how to send a sequence of bits to the adder. A list of bits seems the most straightforward way, with one little twist. Since the addition begins with the least significant bit, and lists are most easily accessed from the front (using first and rest), it would seem helpful if the lists of bits were in the reverse order of the bits as they appear in the usual binary representation; i.e., the binary number 10011 will be represented in SCHEME by the list (|1| |1| |0| |0| |1|).

The function to add two such lists of bits will be recursive. Our approach will be to define a function that adds the first bits of each list (with the appropriate carry-in) and then calls itself recursively on the rest of each list. When we reach the end of a list of digits, we can assume that the next digit is a 0, since we can always add leading zeros to a binary number. (Recall that the digits have been reversed, so that the end of the list corresponds to the beginning of the binary number represented.) The following function implements this stage of the adder.

```scheme
(define (add-bit-lists n1 n2 carry-in)
  (cond ((and (null? n1) (null? n2))
         (list carry-in))
        ((null? n1)
         (cons (full-adder-sum
                 '|0| (first n2) carry-in)
               (add-bit-lists
                 '()
                 (rest n2)
                 (full-adder-carry
                   '|0| (first n2) carry-in))))
        ((null? n2)
         (cons (full-adder-sum
                 (first n1) '|0| carry-in)
               (add-bit-lists
                 (rest n1)
                 '()
                 (full-adder-carry
                   (first n1) '|0| carry-in))))
        (else
         (cons (full-adder-sum
                 (first n1) (first n2) carry-in)
               (add-bit-lists
                 (rest n1)
                 (rest n2)
                 (full-adder-carry
                   (first n1) (first n2) carry-in)))))))
```

Now, perhaps, we can turn our attention to some nice top-level formatting for the user. We need a way to convert normally written binary numbers to lists of bits. One way is to take advantage of the SCHEME function explode, which returns a list of the symbols whose names are the individual characters in the name of (the value of) its argument, for example:

```scheme
[1] (explode 'foo)
(F O O)
[2] (explode 1011)
(|1| |0| |1| |1|)
[3] _
```

Once this function gives us our list of digits, we need to reverse each list, call add-bit-lists with the reversed lists and an initial carry-in of 0, reverse the result, and put it back into a form resembling a standard binary number. We can accomplish all but the last of these with the following simple function:

```scheme
(define (adder n1 n2)
  (reverse
    (add-bit-lists (reverse n1) (reverse n2) '|0|)))
```

The conversion to standard binary form is not quite so easy, however. SCHEME does provide a function, `implode`, but it returns a symbol rather than the number that we would like.

```
[3] (implode (explode 1011))
|1011|
[4] _
```

We must next convert the symbol |1011| to the number 1011. We must make this conversion indirectly in SCHEME by first converting the symbol to a string and then converting that string to a number. The SCHEME functions we need are `symbol->string` and `string->number`. The function `string->number` takes two additional arguments after the string to be converted. The first of these indicates whether the resulting number is to be "exact" (indicated by `'e`) or "inexact" (indicated by `'i`). Currently, PC SCHEME supports only inexact numbers. The second extra argument indicates the number base for the string: `'b` for binary, `'d` for decimal, `'o` for octal, and `'x` for hexadecimal. The resulting number is always assumed to be decimal, so if we indicate binary (`'b`), 1011 will be converted to the equivalent decimal number 11. To make our results look correct, we will lie to the system and tell it our strings are decimal representations, thus preventing any such conversions. The final top-level function is:

```
(define (add n1 n2)
  (string->number
    (symbol->string
      (implode (adder (explode n1) (explode n2))))
    'i
    'd))
```

The following example illustrates the use of our add function. Later we will extend it to accept an arbitrary number of arguments, like the built-in function +.

```
[4] (add 1 1)
10
[5] (add 10011 110)
11001
[6] (add 0 0)
0
[7] (add 1111111111111111111111111111 1)
10000000000000000000000000000
[8] (add 100100101001011111101001 10000111111110101011)
10100011100101110010100
[9] _
```

CHAPTER 6

Recursion and Lists

6.1
WORKING WITH LISTS

In Chapter 4, we discussed the use of recursion to implement repetition in SCHEME. We now look at some more complex uses of recursion on the primary data structures of SCHEME: lists. We have already seen how to define a function which returns the top-level length of a list (`list-length`) and one which prints the successive elements of a list (`write-list`). Both functions use as the base case for the recursion the test (`null?` L). We shall see that this is very common in list processing.

The next few examples deal with functions that act on lists of numbers. The first function we will write will be a simple Boolean test of membership in such a list.

```
(define (member-of-list x L) ...)
```

The recursion will have two base cases:

1. If the list is empty, we know that x *is not* a member of L.
2. If the first element of the list = x, then we know that x *is* a member of L.

The recursive case is taken when neither of the above is true:

3. Since x does not equal the first element of L, we must check the rest of L. x is in L if and only if x is in the *rest* of L.

In SCHEME, our definition becomes:

```
(define (member-of-list x L)
  (cond ((null? L) #F)
        ((= x (first L)) #T)
        (else (member-of-list x (rest L)))))
```

Note that in the final `cond` clause, we simply return the value of (`member-of-list x (rest L)`), based upon our analysis in (3) above.

For our next example, consider a function that calculates the sum of the squares of the numbers in a list. Again, thinking recursively, we note that for non-empty lists, we simply need to add the square of the first number to the sum of the squares of the numbers in the rest of the list. We will also make use of the function sqr, which was defined in Chapter 3.

```
(define (sum-of-squares L)
  (if (null? L)
      0
      (+ (sqr (first L)) (sum-of-squares (rest L)))))
```

The pattern should be becoming clear by now: we use the empty list as a base case and break the list into first and rest for the recursion.

With many recursive functions, we have to build a list to be returned. Such is the case with a function that makes a copy of a given list, as follows:

```
(define (copy-list L)
  (if (null? L)
      '()
      (cons (first L) (copy-list (rest L)))))
```

or a function that substitutes one value for another in a list, such as:

```
(define (substitute old new L)
  (cond ((null? L) '())
        ((= (first L) old)
         (cons new (rest L)))
        (else
         (cons (first L)
               (substitute old new (rest L))))))
```

Compare this with the way it might be done in Pascal:

```
type
     list_ptr  : ^list_node;
     list_node : record
                       first : integer;
                       rest  : list_ptr
                 end;

procedure substitute ( old, new : integer;
                       var L : list_ptr );
     begin
          if L <> nil
            then
                 if L^.first = old
                   then L^.first := new
                   else substitute(old,new,L^.rest)
     end;
```

In the Pascal procedure, we use an assignment to change the old value to the new— a side effect. (Of course, we could write a Pascal function that did not use side effects, but the above procedure is probably the more common choice.) Thus in the final **else** case, we can simply make a recursive call to the function to process the rest of the list. However, in SCHEME, we would lose the front of the list if we didn't cons the first element onto the result of substituting new for old in the rest of the list. The SCHEME function does not change the list it is sent, but rather it returns a new list in which the substitution has been made.

6.2
USING HELPER FUNCTIONS

Sometimes we will want (or even need) to define auxiliary "helper" functions to complete a task. The SCHEME function reverse, which returns a list in reverse order, is an example of a function that could be defined with or without a helper. First without a helper:

```
(define (reverse1 1st)
  (if (null? 1st)
      '()
      (append
        (reverse1 (rest 1st))
        (list (first 1st))))))
```

The function append requires a traversal of its argument list each time it is called. This means that reverse1 would do several traversals of 1st before completing and would be quite slow on long lists.

As an alternative, consider this version of reverse that uses a helper, rev. rev introduces the new parameter, 1st2, which is used to accumulate the elements of 1st1 in reverse order as 1st1 is traversed the first and only time. We might consider defining rev within the body of reverse2 as follows:

```
(define (reverse2 1st)

  (define (rev 1st1 1st2)
    (if (null? 1st1)
        1st2
        (rev (rest 1st1) (cons (first 1st1) 1st2))))

  (rev 1st '()))
```

PC SCHEME allows the above definition. However, the "Revised[3] Report on the Algorithmic Language SCHEME" [SCHEME[3], 1986] states that define is valid "only at the top-level of a <program> and, in some implementations, at the beginning of a <body>." (Apparently, PC SCHEME is one of those implementations.) In the above, the function rev has been defined at the beginning of the body of the definition of reverse2. In this case, rev will be added to the local environment (within reverse2) and not to the top-level environment. As such, rev cannot be called outside of reverse2. SCHEME is a *lexically* scoped language (unlike many earlier versions of LISP that were *dynamically* scoped), and variables and functions introduced within the definition of another function are limited to use within that enclosing function.

We may also use a form of let to introduce local functions, since functions are first-class objects in SCHEME and can be manipulated as any other values. This technique is valid in all implementations of SCHEME. Because rev is a recursive function, we will need letrec in this case.

```
(define (reverse2 lst)
  (letrec ((rev
             (lambda (lst1 lst2)
               (if (null? lst1)
                   lst2
                   (rev
                     (rest lst1)
                     (cons (first lst1) lst2)))))))
    (rev lst '())))
```

letrec evaluates the body of reverse2—(rev lst '())—in a lexical environment that has been extended to include the definition of the helper function rev. The effect in the case of letrec is very similar to the above use of define.

6.3
FUNCTIONS ACCEPTING AN ARBITRARY
NUMBER OF ARGUMENTS—II

In Chapter 3, we introduced the syntax for defining functions that can accept an arbitrary number of arguments. At that time, we mentioned that processing more advanced than we had covered so far was required. We are now ready to look at some more interesting examples of such functions.

In some versions of LISP, the addition function + is defined for only two arguments. While this is not the case in SCHEME, we can approximate the situation by defining a new function, plus2, which does take only two arguments and returns their sum, as follows:

```
(define (plus2 a b) (+ a b))
```

We will now show how to extend such a function to a general function, plus, which acts like the SCHEME +.

Our first, but unfortunately incorrect, attempt might be:

```
(define (plus . arg-list)
  (if (null? arg-list)
      0
      (plus2
        (first arg-list)
        (plus (rest arg-list)))))
```

The basic logic is correct—we use our two-argument plus2 to add the first of the arguments to the value returned by a recursive call to plus on the rest of the argument list. We also define the sum of an empty list of arguments to be zero. The problem is that the function plus that we are defining expects some number of numeric arguments, and not a list of numbers as we are trying to pass to it in the recursive call (plus (rest arg-list)). That is, we should call plus as:

```
(plus 2 3 4 6)
```

and not:

```
(plus '(2 3 4 6))
```

The answer to our dilemma is the SCHEME function apply. apply does just what we need—it takes two arguments, the first a function and the second a list, and returns the result of calling the function with the elements of the list as arguments. So our (correct) definition becomes:

```
(define (plus . arg-list)
  (if (null? arg-list)
      0
      (plus2
        (first arg-list)
        (apply plus (rest arg-list)))))
```

apply gives us the ability, along with eval, to build code and then execute it—a very powerful feature of LISP-like languages.

6.4
EXTENDING OUR RIPPLE-CARRY ADDER

In Chapter 5, we defined a function add that performed binary addition of two arguments. We are now ready to extend this function to accept any number of binary number arguments. To carry this out, we will first define a new function, multi-adder, which extends our previous bit-list function adder to arbitrarily many arguments.

```
(define (multi-adder . list-of-binary-numbers)
  (if (null? list-of-binary-numbers)
      (list '|0|)
      (adder
        (first list-of-binary-numbers)
        (apply
          multi-adder
          (rest list-of-binary-numbers)))))
```

As you can see, this is a simple modification of plus above.

The next step is a little more tricky. It involves redefining the function add so as to have it call multi-adder appropriately. Recall the old definition of add:

```
(define (add n1 n2)
  (string->number
    (symbol->string
      (implode (adder (explode n1) (explode n2))))
    'i
    'd))
```

We run into trouble when we find we have to call explode on each of the arguments provided, though we do not know how many there will be. Again SCHEME provides the answer, in the form of "mapping" functions. The function map takes two arguments, a function and a list, and applies the function to each of the elements of the list. It returns a list of the results. The function for-each introduced in Chapter 4 is also a mapping function, which performs the same function applications as map but which always returns #T. Using map, we come up with the following definition for add:

```
(define (add . list-of-binary-numbers)
  (string->number
    (symbol->string
      (implode
        (apply
          multi-adder
          (map explode list-of-binary-numbers))))))
      'i
      'd))
```

We can now perform the following calculations:

```
[1] (add 1 1 1 1 1)
101
[2] (add 10010 11101 11 11000 1)
1001011
[3] (add)
0
[4] (add 1)
1
[5] _
```

CHAPTER 7

Program Design

In this chapter, we will take a look at some techniques for designing and organizing SCHEME programs. For those who are more familiar with the traditional structured languages such as Pascal, Modula-2, or Ada, SCHEME's organization may seem a bit unsettling. We have seen how we may nest procedures as in Pascal. But languages such as Ada and Modula-2 have begun to stress a new type of program structure. The more recent emphasis in programming has been on modularization, encapsulation of data abstractions, and information hiding. In this chapter, we take a look at these issues in the SCHEME programming environment.

7.1
BLOCK STRUCTURE

In Chapter 5, we developed a function, solve-equation, that returned a list of the real solutions to the equation:

$$ax^2 + bx + c = 0$$

Our function used several helper functions, such as solve-linear-equation, solve-quadratic-equation, find-one-solution, find-two-solutions, and discriminant. In Pascal, we might nest these helper functions within the definition of solve-equation. We can do same in SCHEME using the techniques presented in the preceding chapter. For readability, the following uses internal calls to define.

```
(define (solve-equation a b c)

  (define (solve-linear-equation a b)
    (if (= a 0)
        '()
        (list (/ (- b) a))))
```

```
(define (solve-quadratic-equation a b c)

  (define (discriminant a b c)
    (- (* b b) (* 4 a c)))

  (define (find-one-solution a b)
    (list (/ (- b) (* 2 a))))

  (define (find-two-solutions a b discrim)
    (let ((two-a (* 2 a))
          (minus-b (- b))
          (discr-root (sqrt discrim)))
      (list
        (/ (+ minus-b discr-root) two-a)
        (/ (- minus-b discr-root) two-a))))

  (let ((discrim (discriminant a b c)))
    (cond ((= discrim 0)
             (find-one-solution a b))
          ((> discrim 0)
             (find-two-solutions a b discrim))
          (else
             '() )))))

(if (= a 0)
    (solve-linear-equation b c)
    (solve-quadratic-equation a b c) ))
```

Of course, we could have used let as follows:

```
(define (solve-equation a b c)

  (let ((solve-linear-equation
          (lambda (a b)
            (if (= a 0)
                '()
                (list (/ (- b) a)))))
        (solve-quadratic-equation
            .
            .
            .
          etc.
```

7.2
MODULARIZATION

The natural form for a SCHEME "program" may be a collection of separately defined functions. These function definitions may be stored in separate files, grouped by whatever criteria seem appropriate. As long as nonlocal variables are avoided, we can maintain a level of independence between these modules. SCHEME also provides the ability to compile functions individually. We do not, however, have the equivalent of the Ada package specification or the Modula-2 DEFINITION MODULE. These equivalents must be provided as documentation by the programmer, in order to ensure proper use of the functions provided in a compiled file.

7.3
DATA ABSTRACTION

While strongly typed languages like Pascal assign a fixed data type to each variable, the types of SCHEME are associated with the data objects. Types are determined at run time, and SCHEME code can test the type of a data object at run time before determining how it should be processed. This allows great flexibility in defining general data manipulation functions beyond the capabilities of many other popular languages. This association suggests that data abstraction might best be handled by an object-oriented approach, as described in Chapter 10. For now, note that the flexibility offered by SCHEME's typing allows us to define a general stack (perhaps implemented as a list), which can contain elements of any and all types. With a few simple function definitions:

```
(define (newstack) '())
(define (empty-stack? s) (null? s))
(define (push x s) (cons x s))
(define (stack-top s)     ;return the top element of s
  (if (null? s)
      (error "Stack underflow.")
      (first s)))
(define (pop s)           ;return s less its top element
  (if (null? s)
      (error "Stack underflow.")
      (rest s)))
```

we can create and manipulate general stacks. Since the type of the first parameter to the push function is unspecified in the function definition, we can push an object of any type onto one of these stacks. However, at this point the five functions above are all top-level functions and are not encapsulated into an abstract data type module in any way. We have no information hiding with regard to the structure of the stack or the implementation of the operations. At this level, the integrity of the data abstraction is left to the programmer and is not language enforced.

7.4
EXAMPLE—BINARY SEARCH TREES

Lists can be used to implement more complex data structures such as trees, graphs, etc. For example, consider a binary search tree represented in SCHEME by a list containing a root value and two subtrees:

<bst> .=. (<item> <bst> <bst>)

interpreted as:

```
<bst> .=. ( <root value> <left subtree> <right subtree> )
```

We might define the following abstract operations on our trees:

```
new.bst : {} → <bst>            ;returns an empty <bst>
empty.bst? : <bst> → <boolean>
root-value.bst : <bst> → <item>
left-child.bst : <bst> → <bst>
right-child.bst : <bst> → <bst>
construct.bst : <item> x <bst> x <bst> → <bst>
```

These functions can be implemented in SCHEME as follows:

```
(define (new.bst) '())
(define (empty.bst? bst) (null? bst))
(define (root-value.bst bst) (first bst))
(define (left-child.bst bst) (second bst))
(define (right-child.bst bst) (third bst))
(define (construct.bst root-value left-child right-child)
  (list root-value left-child right-child))
```

Let us next define a search function for our binary search trees. For simplicity, we shall just have it return a Boolean result.

```
(define (search.bst bst value-sought)
  (cond ((empty.bst? bst)
          #F)
        ((= value-sought (root-value.bst bst))
          #T)
        ((< value-sought (root-value.bst bst))
          (search.bst
            (left-child.bst bst) value-sought))
        (else
          (search.bst
            (right-child.bst bst) value-sought))))
```

This is a fairly straightforward extension of our earlier function member-of-list. In this extension, as before, we can simply return the value returned by the recursive call(s).

We may also want a function to insert values into our binary search tree:

```
(define (insert.bst new-value bst)
  (cond ((empty.bst? bst)
          (construct.bst
            new-value
            (new.bst)
            (new.bst)))
        ((= new-value (root-value.bst bst))
          bst)
        ((< new-value (root-value.bst bst))
          (construct.bst
            (root-value.bst bst)
```

```
        (insert.bst
          new-value
          (left-child.bst bst))
        (right-child.bst bst)))
     (else
       (construct.bst
         (root-value.bst bst)
         (left-child.bst bst)
         (insert.bst
           new-value
           (right-child.bst bst)))))))
```

Note the need in the two recursive cases to construct the tree that is to be returned. It is not uncommon to see a programmer who is more used to imperative style programming omit this step and write the last clause, for example, as:

```
   .
   .
   .
(else
  (insert.bst
    new-value
    (right-child.bst bst))) ...
```

In the usual case, where new-value is not already in the tree, this clause would always return what is returned by the first case, i.e., a tree with the new-value at the root and empty subtrees.

7.5
MACROS

PC SCHEME provides for the definition of *macro* forms, which provide for code replacement at run time. A PC SCHEME macro identifies with a symbol (to be used in function position in a list) a function defining a piece of SCHEME code to be substituted for the original macro call before evaluation. Thus, rather than defining sqr as a function (see Chapter 3), we might make sqr a macro as follows:

```
(macro sqr
  (lambda (e)
    (list '* (second e) (second e))))
```

When we call (sqr 3), for example, the entire expression (sqr 3) is passed to the parameter e. The body of the lambda expression builds the code (* 3 3), which is then substituted for (sqr 3) at the point where (sqr 3) was called. The new code, (* 3 3), is then evaluated, and its value is returned as the value of the macro call (sqr 3).

Macros allow the same enhancements to modularization and readability as functions, but with the increased performance generated by the fact that compiled functions containing macro calls will have the macro substitution already in place and will no longer need the extra function call. That is, the first time a macro is called may require extra processing, but later calls (other than at top level) will be faster.

Macros also provide us with the capability of defining new *special forms*—i.e., forms that do not evaluate some or all of their arguments. Thus we can use macros to define new control structures and to simplify top-level user interfaces.

Before we look at some applications of macros, we will introduce two techniques for simplifying their definition. The first is the quasiquote form. The single back-quote (`) can be used to quote expressions in the same way that the normal apostrophe can. Thus `a evaluates to A just as 'a does. However, within the scope of quasiquote, we may escape the effect of the quoting so as to evaluate parts of the expression. The comma (,) is used to indicate an expression that is to be evaluated ("unquoted")—the value is to be inserted into the quasiquoted expression in the location of the comma expression. If the result of the evaluation is a list, and we want the list spliced into the quasiquoted expression, the combination ,@ is used for unquoting. The following brief transcript demonstrates each of these situations.

```
[1] `a
A
[2] `(a ,(cons 'b 'c))
(A (B . C))
[3] `(a ,(list 'b 'c))
(A (B C))
[4] `(a ,@(list 'b 'c))
(A B C)
[5] _
```

Using quasiquote, we can rewrite our sqr macro as follows:

```
(macro sqr
  (lambda (e)
    `(* ,(second e) ,(second e))))
```

We can write a plus macro as follows:

```
(macro plus
  (lambda (e)
    `(+ ,@(rest e))))
```

Notice that the call to (plus 2 3 4) would be replaced by the code (+ 2 3 4) before evaluation.

While quasiquote has improved macro readability (and writeability) to some extent, the explicit reference to e can still be confusing at first. However, we can write a macro, define-macro, which introduces a more familiar structure to macro definitions. The source code for define-macro is given in Appendix B. Using define-macro, we can redo each of the above macro definitions as follows:

```
(define-macro (sqr x)
  `(* ,x ,x))
```

```
(define-macro (plus . lst)
  `(+ ,@lst))
```

Since macros do not evaluate their arguments unless specifically told to do so in the expander (lambda (e) ...), we can use them to define new control structures that conditionally evaluate expressions. For example, we might want a form (unless *<test> <expression>*) that evaluates *<expression>* unless *<test>* is true (i.e., only when *<test>* is false). This is a simple task for a macro:

```
(define-macro (unless test expr)
  `(if (not ,test) ,expr))
```

but would be a problem as a normal function, because expr would be evaluated when the function is called, whether or not the test is true. Our new macro can be used as follows:

```
[20] (let ((x -9))
       (unless (negative? x) (writeln (sqrt x)))
       'done)
DONE
[21] (let ((x 9))
       (unless (negative? x) (writeln (sqrt x)))
       'done)
3.
DONE
[22] _
```

Macros can also be valuable when writing top-level forms for the user interface to SCHEME functions. For example, if we find that entering the quotes around the filename when using load becomes tedious, we could define the following macro loadf (for "load file"):

```
(define-macro (loadf filename)
  `(load ,(symbol->string filename)))
```

which could then be called as:

```
(loadf prog.s)
```

and would do the same thing as:

```
(load "prog.s")
```

The quasiquote (`), unquote (,), and splice-unquote (,@) can be used with any combination of SCHEME forms, including the quote (') itself, as in the following macro, somewhat obscure at first glance, which simply returns its argument without evaluation (like quote).

```
(define-macro (my-quote x) `',x)
```

Macros are very powerful tools, and as such can have dire consequences if used improperly. A problem to watch out for arises when the expression to be expanded has as a nonlocal variable a symbol that is used in the expander function.

Macros are not part of the official definition of the SCHEME language, but are included in many implementations. They have been around in the LISP community for a long time, and their usefulness has prompted their continued inclusion.

CHAPTER 8

File I/O

Up to this point, we have concentrated primarily on the design of interactive SCHEME functions to perform desired calculations, with input restricted to the arguments passed to our functions and with little concern about the form of the value returned. Exceptions to this pattern are found in the print loops of Chapter 4 and the final output of our equation-solving program in Chapter 5. Even these exceptions did not concern themselves with alternative sources of input and produced only screen output. In this chapter, we turn our attention to files as sources of input and destinations for the output of our SCHEME functions.

8.1
SIMPLE FILE I/O

The procedures display, writeln, and newline, introduced in Chapter 5, were used to produce humanly readable output to the screen. A simple SCHEME procedure, called with-output-to-file, allows us to redirect this same output to a specified file. It takes as its two arguments a filename and a parameterless procedure (called a *thunk* in SCHEME). For example, we might wish to send the output of our quadratic-solving program to a file called "solution.txt", with an appropriate heading. The following function does just this.

```
(define (solutions-to-file a b c)
  (with-output-to-file "solution.txt"
    (lambda ()
      (writeln
        "Given the quadratic equation with coefficients:")
      (newline)
```

```
(display "    a = ") (writeln a)
(display "    b = ") (writeln b)
(display "    c = ") (writeln c)
(print-solutions (solve-equation a b c)))))
```

Each of the output procedures sends its output to the specified file while in the environment of the body of the thunk, including the output procedures used within the definition of print-solutions. A call to (solutions-to-file 1 3 -2) would generate the output file:

```
Given the quadratic equation with coefficients:

    a = 1
    b = 3
    c = -2

The real solutions are:

    x = 0.56155281280883
    x = -3.56155281280883
```

The primary input function of SCHEME is read, which returns the next SCHEME expression entered at the keyboard. We can use it to write an equation-solving procedure that prompts for the values of the coefficients, as follows:

```
(define (prompt-and-solve)
   (define (get-coeff coeff-name)
    (begin
      (display "Enter the value of ")
      (display coeff-name)
      (display ":  ")
      (read)))
   (let* ((a (get-coeff "a"))
          (b (get-coeff "b"))
          (c (get-coeff "c")))
     (solve a b c)))
```

Within the procedure get-coeff, the call to (read) returns the value entered at the keyboard, and this value is returned to be bound to the appropriate let* variable. (A better version of this procedure would surely include more descriptive prompts; the above is somewhat simplified for clarity of structure.)

Using the SCHEME procedure with-input-from-file, we may provide a file to be used for input to the read function, in a similar manner to the above output redirection. Two additional problems must be dealt with regarding file input, however: (1) the input file may not exist, and (2) the end of the file may be reached prematurely during an attempt to read. SCHEME provides the functions file-exists? and eof-object? to recognize these situations. Their use is demonstrated in the following procedure, which simply reads all the SCHEME expressions in a given file and "pretty-prints" them on the screen (see Appendix D), each starting on a separate line.

```
(define (display-file filename)
   (define (echo)
    (let ((expr (read)))
      (if (eof-object? expr)
```

```
        (begin
           (newline)
           (display "===== End of file:  ")
           (display filename)
           (writeln " =====")
           (newline))
        (begin
             (pp expr)
             (newline)
             (echo)))))
     (if (file-exists? filename)
       (with-input-from-file filename
          (lambda ()
            (newline)
            (display "===== Contents of ")
            (display filename)
            (writeln " =====")
            (newline)
            (echo)))
        (writeln "No such file."))
      *the-non-printing-object*)
```

An alternative version of this procedure, which uses an iterative looping construct introduced in the next chapter, is given in Appendix B.

At this point, we should mention that the output procedures used so far have been designed to produce output for humans. SCHEME also provides some output procedures that produce output in a form more readable by the read function—with strings enclosed in double quotes and special characters, such as the double quote, escaped using a backslash. Two of the more commonly used of these procedures are:

(write <expr>)   Prints the value of <expr> in machine-readable form
(print <expr>)   Prints the value of <expr> using write, preceded by a (newline)
                   and followed by a space

8.2
I/O PORTS

An alternative to the above is to use the SCHEME procedures call-with-input-file and call-with-output-file. These procedures also take two arguments: a filename and a procedure of only one parameter, as follows:

(call-with-input-file <filename-string> <proc>)
(call-with-output-file <filename-string> <proc>)

When <proc> is evaluated, its parameter is bound to a *port* that has been assigned the file designated by <filename-string>. Each of the I/O procedures that we have covered so far (except for writeln, which always uses the currently active output port) actually takes an additional optional argument, which must be a port. Thus, (display x p) would display the value of x to the port p. A procedure to output the value of its first (numeric) argument, as well as its square, to a file whose name is the second (string) argument, would take the following form:

```
(define (values-to-file x filename)
  (call-with-output-file filename
    (lambda (p)
      (display x p)
      (newline p)
      (display (* x x) p)
      (newline p))))
```

For even more flexibility, we can open any number of files using the procedures `open-input-file`, `open-output-file`, and `open-extend-file` (which opens a file for appending of information). These procedures all take a string representing a filename as their only argument, and return a port, which usually must be bound to a variable for future use. Ports can be closed using the procedures `close-input-port` and `close-output-port`. The following procedure would distribute the expressions from a given source file to two output files, sending atoms to one file and nonatomic expressions to the other.

```
(define (split-file source-file atom-file list-file)
  (define (split source atoms non-atoms)
    (let ((expr (read source)))
      (if (not (eof-object? expr))
          (begin
            (if (atom? expr)
                (print expr atoms)
                (print expr non-atoms))
            (split source atoms non-atoms)))))
  (let ((source-port (open-input-file source-file))
        (atom-port (open-output-file atom-file))
        (list-port (open-output-file list-file)))
    (split source-port atom-port list-port)
    (close-input-port source-port)
    (close-output-port atom-port)
    (close-output-port list-port)))
```

We may also open and close files/ports at top level by using `define` to bind ports to variables, as in:

```
(define in-port (open-input-file "prog1.dat"))
(read in-port)
(close-input-port in-port)
```

8.3
PRINTER OUTPUT

Output to the printer is handled as any other port in PC SCHEME, by using the filename "prn". This technique can be used with any of the output options described above.

8.4
TRANSCRIPTS OF SCHEME SESSIONS

PC SCHEME provides the capability to record a transcript of a session by sending a copy of all console input and output to a specified file. This capability can prove handy when unusual results occur that you would like to study at length after ending your session or take to an instructor for explanation. It is also helpful if you want to produce printed demonstrations of program runs, a technique that was used heavily in this text to produce the actual SCHEME runs.

The procedures needed are transcript-on, which takes a single filename argument, and transcript-off, which takes no argument. Once (transcript-on *<filename>*) has been evaluated, a copy of all information shown on the screen is duplicated in the file *<filename>*, until (transcript-off) is evaluated.

Transcripts are often used to demonstrate the running of a sequence of SCHEME evaluations that may have been planned in advance. Rather than entering each form while transcripting is active and risk error messages due to keyboarding errors, it would be nice to use a text editor to preenter the forms in a file and then to give a command to "run" that file. Just such a procedure is included in Appendix B. It is called demo and takes one argument, which is a filename string. It then reads each SCHEME expression in the file, one at a time in sequence, displays it on the screen, evaluates it, and displays the result. Special prompts are included of the form [Dn], where n is a positive integer, to maintain a similarity to a normal SCHEME interaction while clearly identifying it as a demonstration.

If we use an editor (such as EDWIN) to create the file "demo.dem" containing the following three SCHEME forms:

```
(+ 2 3)
(cons 'a 'b)
(positive? (- 5 2))
```

we can then use demo as follows:

```
[1] (transcript-on "demo.tr")
OK
[2] (demo "demo.dem")

===== Beginning of demo:  demo.dem =====

[D1] (+ 2 3)
5
[D2] (CONS (QUOTE A) (QUOTE B))
(A . B)
[D3] (POSITIVE? (- 5 2))
#T

===== End of demo:  demo.dem =====

[3] (transcript-off)
OK
[4] _
```

The transcript file "demo.tr" will contain:

```
OK
[2] (demo "demo.dem")

===== Beginning of demo:   demo.dem =====

[D1] (+ 2 3)
5
[D2] (CONS (QUOTE A) (QUOTE B))
(A . B)
[D3] (POSITIVE? (- 5 2))
#T

===== End of demo:   demo.dem =====

[3] (transcript-off)
```

The procedure demo provides a good example of the use of file I/O. The source code for demo is included in Appendix B. Note that expressions entered as 'a in our file are displayed as (quote a) by demo. The apostrophe symbol is read-time macro automatically converted to a call to quote by the SCHEME Listener. To display in the short ('a) form would require some extra symbol processing in the procedure that does the writing for demo (see Appendix B for further comments along these lines).

CHAPTER 9

Imperative Programming in SCHEME

While primarily a functional language, SCHEME also provides several syntactic constructs supporting an imperative programming style. These constructs include equivalents of the assignment statement and iterative loops.

9.1
SEQUENCING

SCHEME provides two special forms for iterative sequencing: `begin` and `begin0`. (The keyword `sequence` is identical to `begin` and is included in PC SCHEME to maintain compatibility with earlier versions.) They each can be followed by an arbitrary number of SCHEME forms to be evaluated, such as:

```
[1] (begin
       (writeln 3)
       (writeln 4)
       (writeln 5))
3
4
5
()
[2] _
```

Each of the `writeln` forms is evaluated, with the side effect that each argument is written to the screen, and in the case of `begin`, the value of the *last* form is returned. With `begin0`, the value of the *first* form is returned. In the above case, the returned value (from `(writeln 5)`) is ().

Both `begin` and `begin0` expect that each of the forms in the sequence to be evaluated is used for side effect, except perhaps for the last or first respectively. The values returned by the other forms are discarded. Such side-effecting functions include the previously encountered I/O expressions and assignment, as discussed next. Recall also that a few other previously encountered SCHEME forms such as cond and let can contain a sequence of forms to be evaluated, and generally return the value of the last of such a sequence.

9.2
ASSIGNMENT

We have been using a type of assignment all along whenever we have defined our own functions. The SCHEME special form define actually assigns a function definition to an identifier. Thus when we evaluated:

```
(define sqr (lambda (x) (* x x)))
```

or equivalently:

```
(define (sqr x) (* x x))
```

we assigned the function definition (lambda (x) (* x x)) to the identifier sqr.

The general purpose of define is to enter a variable into the current environment and (usually) to initialize its value. We can use it as above to define function names or to define simple variables, such as:

```
(define x 3)
```

which creates the variable x and assigns it the value 3. We can also use:

```
(define x)
```

to enter x into the current environment without initializing it.

Actually, this is no different from our previous definition of functions, since SCHEME treats functions such as (lambda (x) (* x x)) as true first-order objects that can be manipulated as values in the same way that we might manipulate other values, such as the 3 above.

Now, what about changing the value of a previously defined variable? define is not the appropriate choice in that it creates a new variable in the current environment. What we want to do is give a new *value* to an already existing variable. This is accomplished with the special form set! (usually pronounced "set bang"). (set! x 4) would change the value of the variable x to 4, but only if x had been previously defined. An error results if we try to use set! on an undefined variable.

Note that both define and set! are special forms that do not behave as normal functions. In both cases, the first of the arguments *is not* evaluated, while the second argument *is* evaluated as in normal functions. Thus, when we say:

```
(set! x (add1 x))
```

the expression (add1 x) is evaluated and its value is assigned to the variable x (and not to the *value* of x). Also, the SCHEME manual states that the value returned by each of these special forms is undetermined. They are used for their side effect and not for the functional values returned.

Finally, note that define and set! interact differently with the current environment. define adds the variable to the current local environment, while set! looks for a variable in the current environment to reassign, and if one is not found, it continues its search in the enclosing environments. Compare the following:

```
[1] (define foo 3)
FOO
[2] (define (f)
        (begin
          (define foo 4)
          (writeln foo)
          (set! foo 5)
          (writeln foo)
          *the-non-printing-object*))
F
[3] (define (g)
        (begin
          (set! foo 6)
          (writeln foo)
          *the-non-printing-object*))
G
[4] foo
3               ; since foo was defined to be 3 in [1]
[5] (f)
4               ; foo is locally defined in f to be 4
5               ; foo is set! to 5 within f
[6] foo
3               ; back at top-level foo is still 3
[7] (g)
6               ; within g foo is set! to 6
[8] foo
6               ; since foo was not defined locally in
                ;   g, the top-level value has been set!
[9] _
```

9.3
LOOPS

The SCHEME special form do is used for general iterative looping constructs. Its syntax is:

```
(do ( (<var> {<init> {<step>} } )
          .
          .
          .
      (<var> {<init> {<step>} } ))
    ( <test> <expr> ... )
    <stmt>
        .
        .
        .
    <stmt> )
```

(The expressions within {} above are optional.)

The *<init>* expressions are evaluated in the current environment of the do form (in undetermined order), and their values are bound to the new local variable *<var>*. Next the *<test>* is evaluated, and if it is true, each of the *<expr>*s is evaluated sequentially and the value of the last is returned as the value of the do form. If there are no *<expr>* forms, the value of the *<test>* is returned.

If the *<test>* evaluates false, each of the *<stmt>* forms is evaluated sequentially, in the extended environment. The values returned are ignored. After the last *<stmt>* is evaluated, the *<step>* expressions are evaluated, in the extended environment, and the corresponding *<var>*s are updated to these new values. Then the *<test>* is re-evaluated and handled as before.

Loop Examples

Example 1. Recall the following loop introduced in Chapter 4.

```
i := 1;
while i <= n do
    begin
        writeln(i);
        i := i + 1
    end;
```

Using do, we can implement this in SCHEME as:

```
(define (print-to-n n)
  (do ((i 1 (+ i 1)))
      ((> i n) *the-non-printing-object*)
      (writeln i)))
```

First the local variable i is initialized to 1. Then the test (> i 1) is performed. If true, the nonprinting object is returned, so as not to clutter the screen. If false, the value of i is written to the screen, i is updated to (+ i 1), and the test is repeated.

Example 2. A sum-of-squares function was described in Chapter 6. In Pascal we might write this as:

```
function sum_of_squares ( L : list_type ) : integer;
(* assume that list_type is a simple linked list *)
(* of integers.                                  *)
var
    sum : integer;
begin
    sum := 0;
    while L <> nil do
        begin
            sum := sum + L^.first;
            L := L^.rest
        end;
    sum_of_squares := sum
end;
```

In SCHEME, this would translate directly to:

```
(define (sum-of-squares L)
  (do ((sum 0))
      ((null? L) sum)
      (set! sum (+ sum (sqr (first L))))
      (set! L (rest L))))
```

Another approach, however, might be:

```
(define (sum-of-squares L)
  (do ((lst  L  (rest lst))
       (sum  0  (+ sum (* (first lst) (first lst)))))
      ((null? lst) sum) ))
```

Note that since all *<step>* forms are evaluated before any reassignment of the <var>s, the expression (+ sum (* (first lst) (first lst)))) uses the previous value of lst, as required. Also, this do loop has no *body*—all the work is done in the initialization, updating, and test.

   Example 3. The actual SCHEME function member is not a Boolean function, but rather returns the first *tail* of its list argument that begins with a given element, that is:

```
(member 3 '(1 2 3 4 3 2 1))    =>   (3 4 3 2 1)
(member 3 '(1 2 4))            =>   ()
```

Equality of the given element and the first of the list is tested using equal?. (The variants memq and memv use eq? and eqv? respectively.) A recursive implementation would be:

```
(define (rec-member x L)
  (cond ((null? L) '())
        ((equal? x (first L)) L)
        (else (rec-member x (rest L)))))
```

or, since in the first clause L = ():

```
(define (rec-member x L)
  (cond ((or (null? L) (equal? x (first L))) L)
        (else (rec-member x (rest L)))))
```

whereas the iterative approach using do would be:

```
(define (iter-member x L)
  (do ((lst L (rest lst)))
      ((or (null? lst) (equal? x (first lst))) lst)))
```

Again, we see a do loop with no body.

9.4
PROPERTY LISTS

Most symbols in SCHEME can be bound to values, as can variables in the majority of programming languages. However, you may have noticed that certain symbols, such as #T and #F, cannot—they are *constants*. In general, symbols are not quite like the variables of other languages. They are objects that can be manipulated in their own right. We can ask not only about the type of the value of a symbol, but also about the type of the symbol itself. And a symbol can be the value of another symbol, for example:

```
[1] (define x 3)
X
[2] (define y 'x)
Y
[3] x
3                      ;the value of x is 3
[4] y
X                      ;the value of y is the symbol X
[5] (number? x)
#T                     ;3 is a number
[6] (number? y)
()                     ;the symbol X is not a number
[7] (symbol? x)
()                     ;the value of X is 3, not a symbol
[8] (symbol? y)
#T                     ;the value of Y is X, a symbol
[9] (symbol? 'x)
#T                     ;X (the value of 'x) is a symbol
[10] (eval y)
3                      ;the value of the value of Y is 3
[11] (number? (eval y))
#T
[12] _
```

Note that the argument to the function eval is evaluated before being passed to eval, which then evaluates the result. So in [10] above, the value of y (i.e., X) is passed to eval, which returns the value of X, that is, 3.

In addition to having a value, a symbol can have a global *property list*. A property list is a list that associates values with various properties, also represented by symbols, such as:

```
(color red size large price 6.95)
```

which associates the value red with the property color, and so forth.

Property lists are similar to the more general notion of *association lists,* which are lists of pairs of the form:

```
((color red) (size large) (price 6.95))
```

in which the second element is said to be "associated" with the first. In SCHEME, we can access the associated values through the functions assoc, assq, and assv. Each of these returns the first pair in the association list (passed as the second argument) whose first element is equal (tested using equal?, eq?, and eqv? respectively) to a given value passed as the first argument; for example:

```
[45] (assq
       'size
       '((color red) (size large) (price 6.95)))
(SIZE LARGE)
[46] _
```

Notice that if we wish to find the value associated with 'size, we must apply the function second to the result of the above.

When we use property lists, some of the extra work is performed automatically. Four SCHEME procedures pertain to property lists. They are:

(putprop *<symbol> <value> <property>*)   Adds the given *<value>* to the property list of *<symbol>*, associating it with *<property>*. Previous values are overwritten. An unspecified value is returned.

(getprop *<symbol> <property>*)   Returns the *<value>* associated with *<property>* in the property list of *<symbol>*.

(remprop *<symbol> <property>*)   Deletes *<property>* and any associated *<value>* from the property list of *<symbol>*. Returns an unspecified value.

(proplist *<symbol>*)   Returns the property list of *<symbol>*.

Thus we can do the following:

```
[1] (define sweater1)
SWEATER1
[2] (proplist 'sweater1)
()
[3] (putprop 'sweater1 'red 'color)
RED
[4] (putprop 'sweater1 'large 'size)
LARGE
[5] (putprop 'sweater1 6.95 'price)
6.95
[6] (proplist 'sweater1)
(PRICE 6.95 SIZE LARGE COLOR RED)
[7] (getprop 'sweater1 'color)
RED
[8] (putprop 'sweater1 'brown 'color)
BROWN
[9] (proplist 'sweater1)
(PRICE 6.95 SIZE LARGE COLOR BROWN)
[10] (getprop 'sweater1 'color)
BROWN
[11] (remprop 'sweater1 'price)
(SWEATER1 SIZE LARGE COLOR BROWN)
[12] (proplist 'sweater1)
(SIZE LARGE COLOR BROWN)
[13] (getprop 'sweater1 'price)
()
[14] _
```

It is important to note that property lists of a symbol are defined *globally*, in contrast to the binding of values to symbols. Local identifiers can be bound to values in a local environment, which are different from values in other environments, without affecting those other values. However, a change to the property list of a symbol in one environment affects that symbol's property list in every other environment, even if the symbol has not been defined in that environment, as is demonstrated below:

```
[1] (define x 3)
X
[2] (putprop 'x 3 'value)
3
[3] X
3
[4] (getprop 'x 'value)
3
[5] (define (foo x)
      (set! x 7)
      (putprop 'x 7 'value)
      (putprop 'y 4 'value)
      (writeln x)
      (getprop 'x 'value))
FOO
[6] (foo 10)
7
7
[7] x
3
[8] (getprop 'x 'value)
7
[9] (getprop 'y 'value)
4
[10]y

[VM ERROR encountered!] Variable not defined in current environment
Y

[Inspect] Quit
[11] _
```

Because of this feature, property lists can be used to store global information that is to be accessed by several functions nested at various levels, without explicitly passing that information as a parameter to each function. The functions can also modify that global information much more easily. Although nonlocal access is generally frowned upon in structured program design, there are situations where it may be appropriate. An example is given in the case study in Chapter 11.

CHAPTER 10

Object-Oriented Programming Using SCOOPS

As object-oriented programming (OOP) becomes more and more popular, many older languages are including object-oriented extensions, and SCHEME is no exception. We will assume that the reader is already familiar with the concepts of OOP, and restrict our discussion to the particular implementation in PC SCHEME. The object-oriented package included with PC SCHEME is called Scheme Object-Oriented Programming System, or "SCOOPS," and is accessed by first loading the file "scoops.fsl". This file loading is accomplished by evaluating (load "scoops.fsl"), assuming that "scoops.fsl" is in the current directory. If not, the full pathname should be given, where because of the use of the backslash for escaping characters in a SCHEME string, you must enter each backslash as \\, for example,

```
(load "c:\\languages\\scheme\\scoops.fsl")
```

The extension .fsl indicates that the file is a "fast-load" file. Such files will not be discussed here. For further information, see the *PC SCHEME User's Guide* [SCHEME, 1987a].

Once loaded, SCOOPS provides functions for defining object classes, with class variables, instance variables, and message-handling methods, and supports multiple inheritance. The PC SCHEME SCOOPS forms include:

define-class	Define a new class
compile-class	Install a class in the proper location in the inheritance tree
define-method	Define a message handler
make-instance	Create an instance of a class
send	Send a message to a SCOOPS object

Also included are several other functions that retrieve information about classes and objects. Perhaps the easiest way to describe SCOOPS is to provide a few examples.

10.1
THE CLASS fraction

For our first example, let us create a SCOOPS class that represents rational numbers, not in decimal form, but rather as the ratio of a numerator and a denominator. We will provide methods for combining such fractions, using standard arithmetic operations, as well as for displaying them in various forms. First we define the class:

```
(define-class fraction
    (instvars numerator denominator)
    (options gettable-variables))
```

This form specifies that the name of the class is fraction and that it contains two instance variables, numerator and denominator. The (options ...) clause in this case indicates that methods should automatically be generated for retrieving the value of the instance variables, i.e., methods get-numerator and get-denominator will be system defined. Other options include settable and inittable. These options will be covered in a later example. We also compile the class at this time to link it as necessary into the inheritance hierarchy. (We are not using inheritance in this example, but since the class would be compiled automatically the first time we create an instance anyway, we might as well do it now.)

```
(compile-class fraction)
```

We are now ready to define some methods for working with fractions. The syntax of the define-method form is:

```
(define-method (<class> <method-name>) (<param> ... )
    <expr> ... )
```

The first and perhaps the most complicated method is to assign a fraction a given value. Rather than simply assigning values to the numerator and denominator, which could result in fractions such as 12/8 and 3/–2, we will store all our fractions in a reduced form with a positive denominator.

```
(define-method (fraction init) (n d)
  (if (and (integer? n) (integer? d))
      (if (zero? d)
          (error
            "Division by zero."
            (list n '/ d))
          (let ((divisor (gcd (abs n) (abs d))))
            (set! numerator (/ n divisor))
            (set! denominator (/ d divisor))
            (if (negative? denominator)
                (begin
                  (set! numerator (- numerator))
                  (set! denominator (- denominator))))
            'ok)
      (error
        "Non-integer numerator and/or denominator."
        (list n d))))
```

In this method, we have two formal arguments, n and d, representing the integers from which the fraction is to be formed. Thus the method body begins with a test to see if, indeed, the actual arguments are integers. If so, and if the proposed denominator is not zero, their greatest common divisor is calculated, using the built-in SCHEME gcd function, and the fraction is reduced by dividing n and d by this divisor. The results are stored in the instance variables numerator and denominator. Next we check to see if the denominator is negative, and if so, we change the signs of both numerator and denominator. Finally, we return a simple 'ok. If at least one of the actual arguments is not an integer, we signal an error, passing an error message and a list of the actual arguments. This initiates the PC SCHEME Inspector as described elsewhere in this text.

Now that we can assign values to our fractions, we may want to be able to display them. We will use the message name display-value, defined as:

```
(define-method (fraction display-value) ()
  (if (or (zero? numerator) (= denominator 1))
      (display numerator)
      (begin
        (display numerator)
        (display "/")
        (display denominator)))
  *the-non-printing-object*)
```

We can also convert the fraction to a floating point number as follows:

```
(define-method (fraction as-float) ()
  (float (/ numerator denominator)))
```

Actually, (/ a b) returns float only if necessary; (/ 4 2) returns the integer 2. So the call to float is added above to guarantee that the method always returns a floating point value.

Next we add some arithmetic relations. Note that we can send messages to other objects, including the argument, from within the body of a method.

```
(define-method (fraction equal-to?) (frac)
  (= (* numerator (send frac get-denominator))
     (* denominator (send frac get-numerator))))

(define-method (fraction less-than?) (frac)
  (< (* numerator (send frac get-denominator))
     (* denominator (send frac get-numerator))))

(define-method (fraction greater-than?) (frac)
  (> (* numerator (send frac get-denominator))
     (* denominator (send frac get-numerator))))
```

(Recall that the denominator is always positive, simplifying the inequality tests.)
Next we add the following operations:

```
(define-method (fraction add) (frac)
  (let ((n1 (send frac get-numerator))
        (d1 (send frac get-denominator))
        (ans (make-instance fraction)))
```

```
        (send ans init
            (+ (* numerator d1) (* denominator n1))
            (* denominator d1))
        ans))

(define-method (fraction subtract) (frac)
  (let ((n1 (send frac get-numerator))
        (d1 (send frac get-denominator))
        (ans (make-instance fraction)))
     (send ans init
        (- (* numerator d1) (* denominator n1))
        (* denominator d1))
     ans))

(define-method (fraction multiply-by) (frac)
  (let ((ans (make-instance fraction)))
     (send ans init
        (* numerator (send frac get-numerator))
        (* denominator (send frac get-denominator)))
     ans))

(define-method (fraction divide-by) (frac)
  (let ((ans (make-instance fraction)))
     (send ans init
        (* numerator (send frac get-denominator))
        (* denominator (send frac get-numerator)))
     ans))

(define-method (fraction negate) ()
  (let ((ans (make-instance fraction)))
     (send ans init (- numerator) denominator)
     ans))

(define-method (fraction invert) ()
  (let ((ans (make-instance fraction)))
     (if (negative? numerator)
         (send ans init
            (- denominator) (- numerator))
         (send ans init denominator numerator))
     ans))
```

Lastly, for now, it might be nice to be able to assign the value of one fraction to another, so we define:

```
(define-method (fraction assign!) (frac)
  (set! numerator (send frac get-numerator))
  (set! denominator (send frac get-denominator))
  'ok)
```

The following demo gives some idea of how this can all work. (See Appendix D for the source code for demo.)

```
[1] (demo "fraction.dem")

===== Beginning of demo:  fraction.dem =====

[D1] (DEFINE X (MAKE-INSTANCE FRACTION))
X
[D2] (DEFINE Y (MAKE-INSTANCE FRACTION))
Y
[D3] (DEFINE Z (MAKE-INSTANCE FRACTION))
Z
[D4] (SEND X INIT 2 3)
OK
[D5] (SEND Y INIT 3 4)
OK
[D6] (SEND Z INIT -4 -6)
OK
[D7] (SEND X DISPLAY-VALUE)
2/3
[D8] (SEND Y DISPLAY-VALUE)
3/4
[D9] (SEND Z DISPLAY-VALUE)
2/3
[D10] (SEND X EQUAL-TO? Y)
()
[D11] (SEND X EQUAL-TO? Z)
#T
[D12] (SEND X LESS-THAN? Y)
#T
[D13] (SEND Z INIT -2 5)
OK
[D14] (SEND X LESS-THAN? Z)
()
[D15] (SEND X AS-FLOAT)
0.666666666666667
[D16] (SEND Y AS-FLOAT)
0.75
[D17] (SEND Z ASSIGN! (SEND X ADD Y))
OK
[D18] (SEND Z DISPLAY-VALUE)
17/12
[D19] (SEND (SEND X SUBTRACT Y) DISPLAY-VALUE)
-1/12
[D20] (SEND (SEND X MULTIPLY-BY Y) DISPLAY-VALUE)
1/2
[D21] (SEND (SEND X DIVIDE-BY Y) DISPLAY-VALUE)
8/9
[D22] (SEND (SEND X NEGATE) DISPLAY-VALUE)
-2/3
[D23] (SEND (SEND Z INVERT) DISPLAY-VALUE)
12/17

===== End of demo:  fraction.dem =====

[2] _
```

10.2
INHERITANCE—COURSE SCHEDULE EXAMPLE

An important feature of object-oriented programming is the concept of *inheritance*. Individual instances are members of classes, which themselves may be subclasses of other higher-level classes. Once a method has been defined for a class, and thus for all instances of that class, it would seem that members of any subclass should also have access to that method, or "inherit" the method. The SCOOPS system does in fact provide for (multiple) inheritance, through the use of the keyword `mixins`. For example, the class definition:

```
(define-class char-set
  (instvars ...)
  (mixins set)
  (options ...))
```

would allow the class `char-set` to inherit all methods and instance variables from the class set. The subclass may also include additional instance variables and methods and may override inherited methods with new local definitions. Again we will use an extended example to demonstrate these techniques.

This time our problem domain will be an area familiar to most college students, that of class schedules. We will write some code to help maintain information on courses and various sections of those courses that may be offered at registration time.

The Classes

First we define the class course:

```
(define-class course
  (instvars
    department   ;the department offering the course
    course-no    ;the course number
    course-name  ;the name of the course
    credit-hrs)  ;the number of credit hours
  (options
    gettable-variables
    inittable-variables))

(compile-class course)
```

The option `inittable-variables` allows us to specify the values of the instance variables at the time we create each instance, for example:

```
(define csc410
  (make-instance course
    'department   "Computing Sciences"
    'course-no    410
    'course-name  "Artificial Intelligence"
    'credit-hrs   3))
```

We will also want a class for sections of courses, which will contain slots for things such as the section number, instructor, time, place, list of students registered, etc. Before we define this, we might note that the list of students might be derived from a more general list class, such as:

```
(define-class name-list
  (instvars
    (members '())      ;a list of strings
    (size 0))          ;the length of the name-list
  (options gettable-variables))

(compile-class name-list)
```

Again we see some new syntax: the instance variables members and size have been given initial values by enclosing them in forms such as:

```
(<var> <init-value>)
```

We can now define our section class as follows:

```
(define-class section
  (instvars
    parent-course      ;the course for which this is
                       ;  a section
    section-no         ;the number of the section
    instructor)        ;the instructor of this section
  (mixins name-list)
  (options gettable-variables inittable-variables))

(compile-class section)
```

In addition to the instance variable listed in the definition, section also inherits the instance variables members and size from the class name-list through the use of the mixins clause. It will also inherit any methods that we might define for name-list.

The Methods

We will define just one simple method for the class course, keeping in mind that by having used the gettable-variables option, the methods get-department, get-course-no, get-course-name, and get-credit-hrs have been provided automatically. The additional method will be used to display all of the information about a course on the screen and should be fairly self-explanatory:

```
(define-method (course print-info) ()
  (begin
    (writeln "-------------------------------------")
    (display "Department......") (writeln department)
    (display "Course number...") (writeln course-no)
    (display "Course name.....") (writeln course-name)
    (display "Credit hours....") (writeln credit-hrs)
    (writeln "-------------------------------------")
    *the-non-printing-object*))
```

We will provide three additional methods for the name-list class: one to insert a new name, one to remove a name, and one to list all of the names. The last of these methods is perhaps the simplest and might be written as:

```
(define-method (name-list print-names) ()
  (for-each writeln members)
  *the-non-printing-object*)
```

For the insert method, we will take a short approach and not bother keeping the names in alphabetical order. Thus we can add a name to a list simply by consing it to the beginning of the list. Of course, if the name is already in the list, we should do nothing. The method below implements these ideas and reports what it has done.

```
(define-method (name-list insert!) (new-name)
  (display new-name)
  (if (memv new-name members)
      (writeln " - already in list.")
      (begin
        (set! members (cons new-name members))
        (set! size (add1 size))
        (writeln " - inserted.")))
  *the-non-printing-object*)
```

The memv function has been used, because we are dealing with a list of strings.

Removing a name will not be quite so easy, because the name to be removed will not necessarily be at the front of the list. We will use a helper function, remove, to handle the details, with the rest of the method looking very similar to insert! above.

```
(define (remove n l)
  (cond
    ((null? l) l)
    ((string=? n (first l)) (rest l))
    (else (cons (first l) (remove n (rest l))))))
```

The question remains where to define this helper function. Since this is the only method that will use it, we choose to define it locally, utilizing letrec.

```
(define-method (name-list remove!) (old-name)
  (letrec
    ((remove
       (lambda (n l)
         (cond
           ((null? l) l)
           ((eqv? n (first l)) (rest l))
           (else
             (cons (first l)
                   (remove n (rest l))))))))
    (display old-name)
    (if (memv old-name members)
        (begin
          (set! members (remove old-name members))
          (set! size (sub1 size))
          (writeln " - removed."))
        (writeln " - not currently in list."))
    *the-non-printing-object*))
```

Finally, we define one additional method for the class section, which displays all section information. Note that we can use the same name as used above for the class course.

```
(define-method (section print-info) ()
  (begin
    (send parent-course print-info)
    (display "Section number..") (writeln section-no)
    (display "Instructor......") (writeln instructor)
    (display "Class size......") (writeln size)
    (writeln "-----------------------------------")
    (writeln "Students:")
    (writeln "---------")
    (print-names)
    (writeln "-----------------------------------")
    *the-non-printing-object*))
```

Two comments should be made here: (1) the instance variable size has been inherited from name-list and can be used exactly like the other instance variables; and (2) the print-names method has also been inherited and is called by the simple procedure call (print-names)—the receiver of this message is assumed to be the current object, referred to as "self" in many object-oriented systems.

A Demonstration

Now, let us see these objects in action. First we define some instances of the classes. For ease of reuse, let us create a file, "sections.s," containing the definitions that follow.

```
(define csc410
  (make-instance course
    'department    "Computing Sciences"
    'course-no     410
    'course-name   "Artificial Intelligence"
    'credit-hrs    3))

(define csc410-01
  (make-instance section
    'parent-course  csc410
    'section-no     1
    'instructor     "R. G. Hull"))
```

Next we will perform a few transactions. Let us again use the demo facility, first creating the demo file "courses.dem" containing the following messages:

```
(send csc410 print-info)
(send csc410-01 insert! "John Smith")
(send csc410-01 insert! "Mary Jones")
(send csc410-01 insert! "Bill Brown")
(send csc410-01 insert! "Sue White")
(send csc410-01 print-names)
(send csc410-01 remove! "Bill Brown")
(send csc410-01 print-names)
(send csc410-01 print-info)
(send csc410-01 get-size)
(send csc410-01 get-instructor)
```

We can now load the necessary files and invoke the demo procedure. We will assume that our class and method definitions are in the file "courses.s".

```
[1] (load "scoops.fsl")
OK
[2] (load "courses.s")
OK
[3] (load "sections.s")
OK
[4] (demo "courses.dem")

===== Beginning of demo:  courses.dem =====

[D1] (SEND CSC410 PRINT-INFO)
----------------------------------------
Department......Computing Sciences
Course number...410
Course name.....Artificial Intelligence
Credit hours....3
----------------------------------------

[D2] (SEND CSC410-01 INSERT! "John Smith")
John Smith - inserted.

[D3] (SEND CSC410-01 INSERT! "Mary Jones")
Mary Jones - inserted.

[D4] (SEND CSC410-01 INSERT! "Bill Brown")
Bill Brown - inserted.

[D5] (SEND CSC410-01 INSERT! "Sue White")
Sue White - inserted.

[D6] (SEND CSC410-01 INSERT! "Bill Brown")
Bill Brown - already in list.

[D7] (SEND CSC410-01 PRINT-NAMES)
Sue White
Bill Brown
Mary Jones
John Smith

[D8] (SEND CSC410-01 REMOVE! "Bill Brown")
Bill Brown - removed.

[D9] (SEND CSC410-01 REMOVE! "Mary Smith")
Mary Smith - not currently in list.

[D10] (SEND CSC410-01 PRINT-NAMES)
Sue White
Mary Jones
John Smith

[D11] (SEND CSC410-01 PRINT-INFO)
----------------------------------------
Department......Computing Sciences
Course number...410
```

```
Course name.....Artificial Intelligence
Credit hours....3
--------------------------------------
Section number..1
Instructor......R. G. Hull
Class size......3
--------------------------------------
Students:
---------
Sue White
Mary Jones
John Smith
--------------------------------------

[D12] (SEND CSC410-01 GET-SIZE)
3
[D13] (SEND CSC410-01 GET-INSTRUCTOR)
"R. G. Hull"

===== End of demo:  courses.dem =====

[5] _
```

CHAPTER 11

Case Study:
A SCHEME Compiler for Karel the Robot

As a symbol manipulation language, SCHEME is an excellent choice for language-processing programs. This chapter is devoted to a large application that will demonstrate these capabilities as well as further use of the concepts presented in the foregoing chapters. Our task will be to write a simple compiler. Our source language will be the robot language developed in the text *Karel the Robot, A Gentle Introduction to the Art of Programming*, by Richard E. Pattis [Pattis, 1981]. For our target language, we will use SCHEME. That is, we will write a SCHEME program to translate Karel programs into SCHEME programs, which can then be run using our SCHEME interpreter.

11.1
KAREL THE ROBOT

Karel is a robot that can move about its own special environment and interact with it in a few simple ways. We first describe Karel's world and then the language for controlling Karel.

Karel's Environment

Karel's physical world is essentially the first quadrant of the two-dimensional plane, with vertical and horizontal "streets" corresponding to (positive) integer values along each axis. Karel can move from intersection to intersection along these streets but cannot leave the first quadrant. The lowest numbered streets are numbered 1 in each dimension; there is no street 0. The directions Karel can move in are referred to as North (positive y direction), South (negative y direction), East (positive x direction) and West (negative x direction).

Karel's world also contains an arbitrary number of arbitrarily placed "walls" that block his movement from one intersection, or "corner," to another. Finally, this world contains "beepers" that may be found in any number on any corner. Karel also possesses a "beeper bag" in which he may carry any number of beepers. Each Karel program must be given an initial configuration of walls and beepers as well as the number of beepers in Karel's beeper bag and his initial position and orientation, before it can be run.

Karel's Operations

Karel's motion is limited to moving forward one "block" at a time (to the next street corner) and turning 90° to the left in place. While Karel cannot in general tell on which corner he is positioned, he can tell which direction (north, south, east, west) he is facing, and he can tell whether or not there is a wall in front, to the left, or to the right of him. Finally, he can determine whether or not there are beepers located at his current corner, though not how many. He has the ability to pick up one beeper at a time and place it in his beeper bag. He can also determine whether or not his beeper bag is empty, and if he has beepers in his bag, he can place one at a time on the ground at his current corner.

In addition, Karel can store and execute a program written in his specific programming language, which is described below. Once a program has been entered, Karel can be turned on and will continue to execute the program until he reaches an instruction to turn himself off or until an error condition occurs, in which case he also shuts himself off (this is an *error shutoff*).

11.2
THE KAREL LANGUAGE

The language for controlling Karel the Robot consists of five primitive instructions and five control structures, and includes the ability to define new instructions (parameterless procedures). There are no variables in the language. For conditional forms, there are 18 Boolean tests that can be performed.

Primitive Instructions

The following descriptions of Karel's primitive instructions are taken from pages 5–7 of *Karel the Robot* [Pattis, 1981].[1]

move   When Karel executes a move instruction, he moves forward one block; he continues to face the same direction. To avoid damaging himself, Karel will not move forward if he sees a wall section or boundary wall between himself and the corner that he would

---

[1]Copyright 1981, by John Wiley & Sons, Inc.; reprinted by permission of John Wiley & Sons, Inc.

move toward. Instead, Karel executes a move instruction in this situation by turning himself off. This action [is] called an *error shutoff*.

turnleft   Karel executes a turnleft instruction by pivoting 90° to the left; thus, Karel remains on the same street corner while executing a turnleft instruction. Because it is impossible for a wall section to block Karel's turn, turnleft cannot cause an error shutoff.

pickbeeper   When Karel executes a pickbeeper instruction, he picks up a beeper from the corner he is standing on and then deposits it in his beeper bag. If he executes a pickbeeper instruction on a beeperless corner, Karel performs an error shutoff. On a corner with more than one beeper, Karel randomly picks up one—and only one—of the beepers and then places it in his beeper bag.

putbeeper   Karel executes a putbeeper instruction by extracting a beeper from his beeper bag and placing it on his current street corner. If Karel tries to execute a putbeeper instruction with an empty beeper bag, he performs an error shutoff.

turnoff   When Karel executes a turnoff instruction, he turns himself off and is incapable of executing any more instructions until he is restarted on another task. The last instruction in every robot program must be a turnoff instruction.

Control Structures

Karel's language includes four control structures that are taken directly from Pascal: IF...THEN..., IF...THEN...ELSE..., WHILE...DO..., and block structuring with BEGIN...END. The fifth control structure is a fixed looping structure using the keywords ITERATE...TIMES.... The syntax of each of these control structures is given in the summary below.

Instruction Definitions

The keywords DEFINE-NEW-INSTRUCTION...AS... are used to introduce new instructions into the Karel language. (See summary below.)

General Program Structure

All Karel programs begin with the keyword BEGINNING-OF-PROGRAM and end with END-OF-PROGRAM. Immediately following the BEGINNING-OF-PROGRAM, there may be any number of new instructions defined. The definitions are followed by the executable portion of the program that begins with BEGINNING-OF-EXECUTION and terminates with END-OF-EXECUTION. Instructions are separated by semicolons, as in Pascal.

Summary

The following summary of the Karel language is taken from Appendix A of [Pattis, 1981].[2]

Robot Programming Summary

Primitive Instructions

1. `move`   Karel moves one block forward.
2. `turnleft`   Karel pivots 90° to the left.
3. `pickbeeper` Karel puts a beeper in his beeper bag.
4. `putbeeper`   Karel places a beeper on the corner.
5. `turnoff`   Karel turns himself off.

Block-Structuring Instruction

6. `BEGIN`

```
        <instruction>;
        <instruction>;

            .    .

            .    .

            .    .

        <instruction>;
        <instruction>
    END
```

Conditional Instructions

7. `IF <test>`
```
        THEN <instruction>
```

8. `IF <test>`
```
        THEN <instruction>
        ELSE <instruction>
```

Repetition Instructions

9. `ITERATE <positive-number> TIMES`
```
        <instruction>
```

10. `WHILE <test> DO`
```
        <instruction>
```

The Mechanism for Defining New Instructions

11. `DEFINE-NEW-INSTRUCTION <new-name> AS`
```
        <instruction>
```

Specifying a Complete Program

12. `BEGINNING-OF-PROGRAM`
```
        DEFINE-NEW-INSTRUCTION <new-name> AS
            <instruction>;
```

```
                .
                .
                .
    DEFINE-NEW-INSTRUCTION <new-name> AS
        <instruction>;

    BEGINNING-OF-EXECUTION
        <instruction>;
            .     .
            .     .
            .     .
        <instruction>
    END-OF-EXECUTION
    END-OF-PROGRAM
```

Bracketed Words

1. `<instruction>`   Any of the robot instructions (1–10)
2. `<new-name>`   Any new word (in lowercase letters, numbers, "-")
3. `<positive-number>`   Any positive number
4. `<test>`   Any of the following:

```
    front-is-clear, front-is-blocked,
    left-is-clear, left-is-blocked,
    right-is-clear, right-is-blocked,
    next-to-a-beeper, not-next-to-a-beeper,
    facing-north, not-facing-north,
    facing-south, not-facing-south,
    facing east, not-facing-east,
    facing-west, not-facing-west,
    any-beepers-in-beeper-bag,
       no-beepers-in-beeper-bag
```

11.3
COMPILER SPECIFICATION

First we must determine just what we want our compiler to do. Of course, it should take as input Karel code and produce some kind of executable code, but we must specify more completely the form of both input and output.

Input

Input to our compiler will be a standard text file containing a Karel program. The Karel program should conform to the language specification above, though we must be able to recognize, and hopefully report on, errors in Karel syntax. A complication arises due to the fact that the semicolon is the comment indicator in SCHEME and would thus require special processing to read. Actually, we may allow semi-colons as statement separators in our Karel source code as long as nothing follows them on their line of text. For simplicity, we will have our compiler just ignore them.

Output

The output of our compiler will be SCHEME expressions that will eventually be passed to an interpreter. That is, our "object code" will consist of a sequence of yet-to-be-defined SCHEME procedures that, when executed in order, will simulate the Karel program. Our compiler need only convert the Karel program into this sequence of syntactically correct SCHEME procedure calls.

11.4
COMPILER IMPLEMENTATION

The structure of the Karel language is given by the state diagrams of Figures 11.1 through 11.3.

To facilitate manipulating the Karel source code, we will first read it into a SCHEME list of the symbols comprising the program and store this list as the value of the property source-program on the symbol karel-compiler. This is all handled by the following procedure:

```
(define (load-karel-program source-file)
  (if (file-exists? source-file)
    (with-input-from-file source-file
      (lambda ()
        (do ((token (read) (read))
             (program '() ))
            ((eof-object? token)
              (putprop
                'karel-compiler
                (reverse program)
                'source-program)
              (display "Program loaded."))
          (set! program (cons token program)))))
    (display "Source file not found.")))
```

Note that the list program is actually built up in reverse order for efficiency and then reversed when put into the property list of karel-compiler.

Now that we have our list of tokens that make up the source program, we need some simple procedures for manipulating it.

```
(define (next-token)
  (first (getprop 'karel-compiler 'source-program)))

(define (consume-token)
  (putprop
    'karel-compiler
    (rest (getprop 'karel-compiler 'source-program))
    'source-program))
```

We will also need information about the predefined words in the Karel language, as well as any user-defined identifiers (of which there are initially none). All this information can also be stored on the property list of `karel-compiler`.

```
(define (initialize-karel-compiler)
  (begin
    (putprop
      'karel-compiler
      '(move turnleft putbeeper pickbeeper turnoff)
      'primitive-instructions)
    (putprop
      'karel-compiler
      '(BEGINNING-OF-PROGRAM BEGINNING-OF-EXECUTION
        DEFINE-NEW-INSTRUCTION END-OF-PROGRAM
        END-OF-EXECUTION WHILE DO ITERATE TIMES AS
        BEGIN END IF THEN ELSE)
      'reserved-words)
    (putprop
      'karel-compiler
      '(front-is-clear front-is-blocked left-is-clear
        left-is-blocked right-is-clear right-is-blocked
        next-to-a-beeper not-next-to-a-beeper
        facing-north not-facing-north facing-south
        not-facing-south facing-east not-facing-east
        facing-west not-facing-west
        any-beepers-in-beeper-bag no-beepers-in-beeper-bag)
      'tests)
    (putprop
      'karel-compiler
      '()
      'user-ids)))
```

`initialize-karel-compiler` should be called at the beginning of any compilation.

We can simplify our task if we provide abstract access functions for the compiler information, such as:

```
(define (primitive-instruction? token)
  (memq token
    (getprop 'karel-compiler 'primitive-instructions)))

(define (reserved-word? token)
  (memq token (getprop 'karel-compiler 'reserved-words)))

(define (test? token)
  (memq token (getprop 'karel-compiler 'tests)))

(define (user-id? token)
  (memq token (getprop 'karel-compiler 'user-ids)))
```

Additionally, we may find the following functions useful:

```
(define (positive-integer? token)
  (and (integer? token) (positive? token)))

(define (end-of-source?)
  (null? (getprop 'karel-compiler 'source-program)))
```

```scheme
(define (save-new-user-id token)
  (putprop
    'karel-compiler
    (cons token (getprop 'karel-compiler 'user-ids))
    'user-ids))
```

We can now write our state transition functions, starting with those for a Karel
<program> as shown in Figure 11.1. The basic pattern is to check the next token,
perhaps consume it, and call the next state function, perhaps consing on some object (SCHEME) code. p0 will eventually return the object code (in list form) for the
entire Karel program.

```scheme
(define (p0)
  (cond ((eq? (next-token) 'BEGINNING-OF-PROGRAM)
         (consume-token)
         (p1))
        (else (error "Missing BEGINNING-OF-PROGRAM"))))

(define (p1)
  (cond ((eq? (next-token) 'DEFINE-NEW-INSTRUCTION)
         (cons (d0) (p1)))
        ((eq? (next-token) 'BEGINNING-OF-EXECUTION)
         (consume-token)
         (p2))
        (else
          (error
            "Expecting BEGINNING-OF-EXECUTION or DEFINE-NEW-INSTRUCTION."))))

(define (p2)
  (cond ((eq? (next-token) 'END-OF-EXECUTION)
         (consume-token)
         (p3))
        (else (let ((instr (s0)))
                (if instr
                  (cons instr (p2))
                  (error "Expecting statement or END-OF-EXECUTION."))))))

(define (p3)
  (cond ((eq? (next-token) 'END-OF-PROGRAM)
         (consume-token)
         (p4))
        (else (error "Expecting END-OF-PROGRAM."))))

(define (p4)
  (if (end-of-source?)
    '()
    (error "Text found following end of program.")))
```

Functions p0, p3, and p4 are fairly straightforward and should pose no problem. p1
and p2 actually do the major work, by calling d0 and s0 respectively. d0 returns the
compiled code for a new instruction definition, and s0 returns the compiled code
for a Karel statement. After calling each of these functions we return to the same p
state, following the loops in the state diagram. The let form is used in p2 to allow
a single call to s0, whose result can be used in two places. If s0 returns '(), there
must have been no more statements in the source code, and since we have already
tested for 'END-OF-EXECUTION, we must have an error.

\<program\>

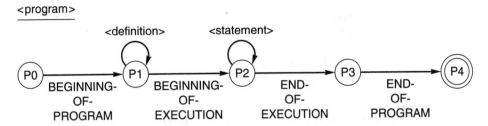

FIGURE 11.1
State diagram for a Karel program

\<definition\>

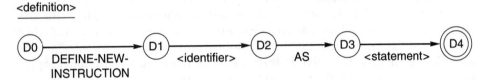

FIGURE 11.2
State diagram for Karel definitions

Let us now look at the state functions for a new definition (Figure 11.2):

```scheme
(define (d0) (begin (consume-token) (d1)))

(define (d1)
  (let ((token (next-token)))
    (cond ((primitive-instruction? token)
           (error
             "Cannot redefine a primitive instruction."
             token))
          ((reserved-word? token)
           (error
             "Cannot redefine a reserved word."
             token))
          ((test? token)
           (error
             "Cannot redefine a test."
             token))
          ((user-id? token)
           (error
             "Instruction already defined."
             token))
          (else
            (save-new-user-id token)
            (consume-token)
            `(define (,token) ,(d2)))))))
```

```
(define (d2)
  (cond ((eq? (next-token) 'AS)
         (consume-token)
         (d3))
        (else (error "Missing AS."))))

(define (d3)
  (cond ((s0))
        (else (error "Improper definition." (next-token)))))
```

Some of these functions deserve a little explanation. d1 starts by ensuring that the identifier chosen for the new definition is valid, and if it is not, it gives an appropriate error message. If the identifier is OK, it is added to the list of user-ids and some object code is generated—in the form of a call to the SCHEME form define. d3 is interesting in that the first cond clause contains only a call to (s0). In the general form for cond, each clause can contain one or more expressions, the first of which is the test. If that test is nonnull, the remaining expressions are evaluated and the last value obtained is returned. In this case, since there are no additional expressions, the value of (s0) is the last value calculated and returned.

The state diagram for Karel statements (Figure 11.3) is certainly the most complex, and will require the most state functions. The pattern should be clear by now,

<statement>

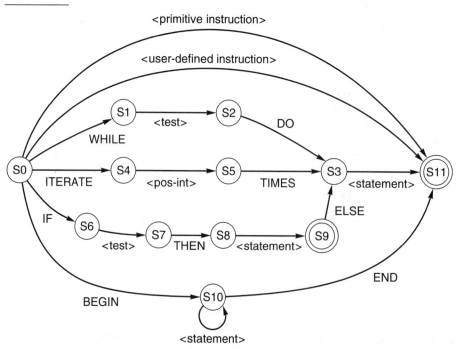

FIGURE 11.3
State diagram for Karel statements

though we should point out that state s3 has been broken into two functions, s3a and s3b, for the sole purpose of separating error messages. Primitive and user-defined instructions will eventually be interpreted by SCHEME functions of the same name. This interpretation could pose a potential problem if a user chooses an identifier that is a predefined SCHEME form, but it is a problem that would not be too hard to deal with in the unlikely case that it were to come up. The Karel forms IF... and BEGIN...END are translated directly into SCHEME equivalents, but WHILE... and ITERATE... require new forms to be defined, called while.k and iterate.k, respectively. (These definitions will be addressed below.) The state functions for Karel statements are:

```
(define (s0)
  (let ((token (next-token)))
    (cond ((primitive-instruction? token)
            (consume-token)
            (list token))
          ((user-id? token)
            (consume-token)
            (list token))
          ((eq? token 'WHILE)
            (consume-token)
            `(while.k ,@(s1)))
          ((eq? token 'ITERATE)
            (consume-token)
            `(iterate.k ,@(s4)))
          ((eq? token 'IF)
            (consume-token)
            `(if ,@(s6)))
          ((eq? token 'BEGIN)
            (consume-token)
            `(begin ,@(s10)))
          (else (error "Unknown instruction." token)))))

(define (s1)
  (let ((token (next-token)))
    (cond ((test? token)
            (consume-token)
            (cons (list token) (s2)))
          (else (error "Invalid test." token)))))

(define (s2)
  (cond ((eq? (next-token) 'DO)
          (consume-token)
          (list (s3a)))
        (else (error "Expecting DO."))))

(define (s3a)
  (cond ((s0))
        (else (error "Invalid loop body."))))

(define (s4)
  (let ((token (next-token)))
    (cond ((positive-integer? token)
            (consume-token)
            (cons token (s5)))
```

```scheme
          (else (error "Expecting a positive integer for ITERATE."
                        `(rather than ,token))))))

(define (s5)
  (cond ((eq? (next-token) 'TIMES)
          (consume-token)
          (list (s3a)))
        (else (error "Expecting TIMES."))))

(define (s6)
  (let ((token (next-token)))
    (cond ((test? token)
            (consume-token)
            (cons (list token) (s7)))
          (else (error "Invalid test." token)))))

(define (s7)
  (cond ((eq? (next-token) 'THEN)
          (consume-token)
          (s8))
        (else (error "Expecting THEN."))))

(define (s8)
  (let ((stmt (s0)))
    (cond (stmt (cons stmt (s9)))
          (else (error "Invalid instruction after THEN.")))))

(define (s9)
  (cond ((eq? (next-token) 'ELSE)
          (consume-token)
          (list (s3b)))
        (else '() )))

(define (s3b)
  (cond ((s0))
        (else (error "Invalid instruction after ELSE."))))

(define (s10)
  (cond ((eq? (next-token) 'END)
          (consume-token)
          '() )
        (else (let ((stmt (s0)))
                (if stmt
                  (cons stmt (s10))
                  (error "Missing END."))))))
```

We have introduced two new SCHEME forms to be used in our object code, and we must now define them. We will implement them as macros.

```scheme
(define-macro (while.k test-fn stmt)
  `(do () ((not ,test-fn) #T) ,stmt))

(define-macro (iterate.k n stmt)
  `(do ((x ,n (sub1 x))) ((zero? x) #T) ,stmt))
```

The compiler is started by simply calling the first state function (p0). Since we might want a more descriptive name for our compiler, we can define:

```
(define (compile-karel-program) (p0))
```

This function will return the object code list.

11.5
BUILDING AN INTERPRETER FOR OUR OBJECT CODE

The heart of our object code interpreter is a single function, run-karel-program. Its main purpose will be to loop through the expressions in the object code, pretty-print them to the screen as a trace of the execution, and evaluate them in sequence using eval. Our program might terminate in three ways: (1) through the normal evaluation of turnoff, (2) due to an error-shutoff, or (3) if the end of the source is reached with no call to turnoff. To control the execution and termination situations, two global variables are defined that are used as flags in run-karel-program:

```
(define run-finished?)
(define completion-code)
```

These variables will be set to appropriate values by run-karel-program and by the functions that implement turnoff and error-shutoff. They then will be tested by run-karel-program, using the SCHEME case form described in Appendix A, to determine a message to report at the end of the run. Finally, run-karel-program will display the final configuration of Karel's world.

```
(define (run-karel-program object-code)
  (begin
    (set! run-finished? #F)
    (do ((obj-code object-code (rest obj-code)))
        ((run-finished? #T)
        (if (null? obj-code)
            (begin
              (set! run-finished? #T)
              (set! completion-code 'no-turnoff))
            (begin
              (pp (first obj-code))
              (newline)
              (eval (first obj-code)))))
    (newline)
    (case completion-code
      ('successful-turnoff
        (writeln "Successful run."))
      ('no-turnoff
        (writeln "No turnoff instruction given."))
      ('error-shutoff
        (writeln "Error shutoff occurred.")))
    (display-world)
    *the-non-printing-object*))
```

Before we can actually run our object code, we must implement in SCHEME the various Karel primitive instructions and tests. These, in turn, will require a representation of Karel's operating environment by some SCHEME structure. However, using a top-down design method, we can delay the representation details as long as we provide access to Karel's position and orientation, the beepers Karel is carrying, and the placement of beepers and wall sections in Karel's world. With this in mind, we begin the (high-level) implementation of the primitive instructions.

```
(define (move)
  (if (front-is-clear)
      (set-karel-position!
        (next-corner (get-karel-orientation)))
      (error-shutoff)))

(define (turnleft)
  (set-karel-orientation!
    (left-dir (get-karel-orientation))))

(define (pickbeeper)
  (cond ((next-to-a-beeper)
          (remove-beeper-from-world
            (get-karel-position))
          (increment-beepers-in-bag 1))
        (else
          (error-shutoff))))

(define (putbeeper)
  (cond ((any-beepers-in-beeper-bag)
          (insert-beeper-in-world
            (get-karel-position))
          (increment-beepers-in-bag -1))
        (else
          (error-shutoff))))

(define (turnoff)
  (begin
    (set! run-finished? #T)
    (set! completion-code 'successful-turnoff)))
```

At this point, we may as well also define error-shutoff:

```
(define (error-shutoff)
  (begin
    (set! run-finished? #T)
    (set! completion-code 'error-shutoff)))
```

Aside from the Karel environment access procedures and a few Karel tests, we have called on two helper functions, next-corner and left-dir. Since these also need some information about the representation of the environment, it seems that we can stall that operation no longer.

The five key components of Karel's environment have already been enumerated: for Karel, there is position, orientation, and beepers carried; and for the world, there is beeper and wall placement. If we choose to represent street intersections in Karel's world by pairs of positive integers, (x y), where, for example, (5 3) represents the intersection of the fifth North-South street and the third East-West street, then we can represent Karel's position by such a pair, the locations of world beepers by a list of such pairs, and the locations of wall sections by a list of pairs of such pairs (each pair of pairs indicating a wall section blocking passage between the two intersections). Karel's orientation can be represented by one of the symbols 'N, 'S, 'E, 'W, and the number of beepers in Karel's bag by a nonnegative integer.

The next question is where to store such information. Following the pattern used in storing key compiler information, we choose to use the property list of a symbol, 'karel-world, storing the required information under the properties position, orientation, beepers-in-bag, beeper-locations, and wall-sections. Thus, we can easily implement the access procedures in the following manner:

```
(define (get-karel-position)
   (getprop 'karel-world 'position))

(define (set-karel-position! new-position)
   (putprop 'karel-world new-position 'position))
```

and so forth.

Beeper manipulations might be handled as:

```
(define (increment-beepers-in-bag n)
   (putprop
     'karel-world
     (+ (getprop 'karel-world 'beepers-in-bag) n)
     'beepers-in-bag))

(define (insert-beeper-in-world posn)
   (putprop
     'karel-world
     (cons posn
           (getprop 'karel-world 'beeper-locations))
     'beeper-locations))

(define (remove-beeper-from-world posn)
   (define (remove1 posn lst)
      (cond ((null? lst) '() )
            ((equal? posn (first lst)) (rest lst))
            (else (cons (first lst)
                        (remove1 posn (rest lst))))))
   (putprop
     'karel-world
     (remove1 posn
              (getprop 'karel-world 'beeper-locations))
     'beeper-locations))
```

The previously mentioned helper functions can now be written:

```
(define (left-dir old-dir)
  (second
    (assq old-dir
          '((N W E) (W S N) (S E W) (E N S)))))

(define (right-dir old-dir)
  (third
    (assq old-dir
          '((N W E) (W S N) (S E W) (E N S)))))

(define (next-corner dir)
  (case dir
    ('N
      (list (first (get-karel-position))
            (add1 (second (get-karel-position)))))
    ('S
      (list (first (get-karel-position))
            (sub1 (second (get-karel-position)))))
    ('E
      (list (add1 (first (get-karel-position)))
            (second (get-karel-position))))
    ('W
      (list (sub1 (first (get-karel-position)))
            (second (get-karel-position))))))
```

The procedure display-world, called by run-karel-program, is quite easy to write and is left as an exercise. All that remains are the many Karel tests. We will show the code for a few key tests, and leave the rest as easy exercises.

```
(define (facing-north)
  (eq? (get-karel-orientation) 'N))
(define (not-facing-north) (not (facing-north)))
```

and so forth.

```
(define (any-beepers-in-beeper-bag)
  (positive? (get-karel-beepers)))

(define (no-beepers-in-beeper-bag)
  (zero? (get-karel-beepers)))

(define (next-to-a-beeper)
  (member (get-karel-position) (get-world-beepers)))

(define (not-next-to-a-beeper)
  (not (next-to-a-beeper)))

(define (front-is-blocked)
  (or (and (= (first (get-karel-position)) 1)
           (facing-west))
      (and (= (second (get-karel-position)) 1)
           (facing-south))
      (member
        (list (get-karel-position)
              (next-corner (get-karel-orientation)))
        (get-world-walls))))
```

```
(member
  (list (next-corner (get-karel-orientation))
        (get-karel-position))
  (get-world-walls)))))
```

```
(define (front-is-clear) (not (front-is-blocked)))
```

`left-is-blocked` and `right-is-blocked` are similar to the above, with changes in the directions tested in the and clauses, and `(next-corner (get-karel-orientation))` replaced by `(next-corner (left-dir (get...)))` or `(next-corner (right-dir (get...)))`, respectively for `left-is-blocked` and `right-is-blocked`.

11.6
USING THE KAREL COMPILER

There are two steps to using the compiler we have developed. First, one must enter a Karel program into a standard text file, say "prog1.k", and then after loading all the pertinent SCHEME files, evaluate:

```
(load-karel-program "prog1.k")
```

We are now ready to compile and run the program, by calling:

```
(run-karel-program (compile-karel-program))
```

If you would rather separate the compiling and running stages, you can save the object code in a top-level variable as follows:

```
(define object-code (compile-karel-program))
```

and then run it as many times as you would like with:

```
(run-karel-program object-code)
```

In addition, you can display the source code file with:

```
(display-text-file "prog1.k")
```

(see Appendix B) and display the object code with:

```
(pp object-code)
```

What we have not provided here is a full set of procedures for initializing Karel environments before running programs. But then, this was not meant to be a commercial system, but rather an example of the symbol manipulation capabilities of SCHEME, along with some program design hints and demonstrations of additional SCHEME procedures. A few parts of this project have been left to the reader, and many nice enhancements are certainly possible for those who wish to explore the SCHEME system further.

CHAPTER 12

Final Remarks

In attempting to keep this text brief, we have covered only a limited selection of the available SCHEME procedures relating to many of the topics discussed, and we have completely omitted several of the advanced features of the SCHEME language. In this chapter, we shall outline a few of these omissions and hopefully in doing so convince the reader that SCHEME is more than just another dialect of LISP, but in fact has many unique features that make it a very interesting language in its own right. Again we refer you to the texts listed at the end of this book, and in particular to the PC SCHEME system available from Texas Instruments, Inc. PC SCHEME is a very complete and robust system and is available at a remarkably low price. It comes highly recommended.

12.1
CHARACTERS, STRINGS, AND SYMBOLS

PC SCHEME comes with a full complement of string and substring manipulating procedures, including the ability to use (read) to access the characters in a string one at a time. Also provided are I/O procedures for individual characters, which would allow us to remove the semicolon restriction placed on us in Chapter 11. Certainly, such a course of action would require more work for us in the parsing of our Karel source program, but the easy conversions between characters, strings, and symbols provided by SCHEME would still make the situation easier than one would find in Pascal-like languages.

12.2
INPUT AND OUTPUT

In addition to the character and string I/O procedures mentioned in the preceding paragraph, SCHEME provides several procedures for testing and manipulating I/O ports, including control over the positioning of the output on a byte level. PC SCHEME also comes with a full set of procedures for manipulating windows and color graphics (not included in standard SCHEME).

12.3
DATA STRUCTURES

In addition to those data structures mentioned previously in this text, SCHEME provides data structuring in the form of *vectors* (somewhat similar to arrays) and *structures* (similar to records) with automatically defined constructors, selectors, and recognizers.

Numeric data structures of standard SCHEME include complex and rational numbers, though these are not implemented in PC SCHEME. For floating point numbers and integers, PC SCHEME provides many additional functions, including the trigonometric functions (sin, cos, tan, asin, acos, atan), logarithmic and exponential functions (log, exp), and random-number generation.

Destructive procedures are also available for modifying lists and pairs. For example, the function append! not only appends lists, but also modifies all but the last one so that they become one long list. Of course, from a functional point of view, these side-effecting procedures are to be avoided. They do improve efficiency in many situations, however.

Procedures and environments are first-class data objects and also come with several procedures for manipulating them. We can access the current and global environments and inspect their bindings, we can create new environments, and we can pass environments explicitly to procedures such as eval.

12.4
ADVANCED DATA STRUCTURES

SCHEME provides a few data objects that are quite different from anything found in the Pascal family of languages. They include *engines* (which execute for a fixed amount of time before returning a value or a new engine), *streams* (with the ability to delay and force evaluation), and *continuations* (which allow us to freeze a computation for completion at a later time). Continuations can also be used to generate nonlocal exits from procedures, which are often handy when encountering special situations deep within a recursion. The *fluid environment* and fluid bindings allow us to define variables that are dynamically rather than lexically scoped.

12.5
CONTROL

In addition to the implicit lazy evaluation provided by forms such as `if` and `cond`, the forms `delay` and `force` provide the programmer with explicit control over lazy evaluation. To `delay` an expression is to define a promise of future evaluation of that expression when such evaluation is needed, i.e., explicitly called for. In order to redeem the promise of the `delay`, we use the function `force`. Once an evaluation has been forced, the resulting value is remembered, so that subsequent calls for that value need not be recalculated.

As an example, consider a function to calculate powers of 2. We could simply calculate each power of 2 as it is requested, which would require redundant calculations for subsequent calls to this function. Or perhaps we might consider building a list of all powers of 2 that we will need, and then simply accessing the appropriate list element when we need a particular power. This approach would require (1) having an upper bound on the powers of 2 that will be needed, and (2) performing many, perhaps unnecessary, calculations when we first create this list. The idea of lazy evaluation is to put off these calculations until they are required. SCHEME provides streams for just this purpose, but for this example, we will create our own stream-like object, `powers-of-2`, which will represent a potential list of the powers of 2, starting with 2^0. Access to the elements of `powers-of-2` will be provided by the functions `hd` and `tl`. (These names are taken from SCHEME's built-in stream functions, `head` and `tail`.) `hd` simply returns the first element, and is defined as equivalent to `car`. The function `tl`, which will return the rest of the elements, must call `force` the `cdr` in order to redeem the promise of the `delay`. The helper function `nth`, similar in purpose to the SCHEME function `list-ref`, uses `hd` and `tl` to return a specified element of our pseudo-stream. We define `powers-of-2`, `hd`, `tl`, and `nth` within the definition of `power2` to prevent their use on inappropriate objects unrelated to this particular problem.

```
(define (power2 n)

  (define powers-of-2
    (letrec ((next
               (lambda (n)
                 (cons n (delay (next (* n 2)))))))
      (next 1)))

  (define hd car)

  (define (tl s) (force (cdr s)))

  (define (nth s n)
    (if (zero? n)
        (hd s)
        (nth (tl s) (-1+ n))))

  (nth powers-of-2 n))
```

The first time power2 is called for a given power n, the necessary calculations will be performed (unless there has been a previous call to power2 for a larger power), and all powers of 2 up to n will be saved for future reference. If n is large, this will involve significant computation, but subsequent calls to power2 for powers less than or equal to n will access the previously calculated values, and will return much faster.

12.6
DOS INTERFACE

PC SCHEME provides a number of procedures that interact with the underlying operating system. These procedures allow for copying, renaming, and deleting files; changing directories or disk drives; returning the size of a file; and returning a list of the files in the current directory. The procedure dos-call executes .exe and .com files with specified arguments.

A Glossary of Commonly-Used SCHEME Procedures

Listed below are many of the more commonly-used SCHEME procedures and functions, including those used in this text. SCHEME is a very full language with many more procedures for manipulation of characters, continuations, engines, environments, pairs and lists, ports, procedures, streams, strings, error handling, debugging, graphics, SCOOPS, etc. For a complete list of SCHEME procedures, see the *TI SCHEME Language Reference Manual* [SCHEME, 1987c].

A.1
DEFINING FORMS

- (define <*variable*> {<*expr*>})

  Define <*variable*> in the current environment and optionally assign it the value of <*expr*>.

- (define (<*function-name*> <*arg*> <*arg*> ...) <*expr*> <*expr*> ...)

  Alternative form of define for defining functions.

- (macro <*macro-name*> <*macro-expander-function*>)

  Define a SCHEME macro. The macro expander function may contain calls to quasiquote (`), unquote (,), and unquote-splicing (,@).

A.2
CONTROL STRUCTURES

- (begin <*expr*> <*expr*> ...)

  Evaluate <*expr*>s in sequence and return the value of the last one. begin0 is structured similarly but returns the value of the first <*expr*>.

- (case <*expr*> <*list*> <*list*> ...)

  Evaluate the <*expr*>, compare its value with the first element of each <*list*> in sequence, and as soon as the comparison returns true, evaluate the remaining expressions in the <*list*>, returning the last value as the value of the case. The first element of each <*list*> must be an atom (in which case eqv? is used for comparison) or a list of atoms (in which case memv is used).

- (cond <*list*> <*list*> ...)

  Evaluate the first element of each <*list*> in sequence, and as soon as a nonnull value is returned, evaluate the remaining elements of that <*list*>, returning the last value as the value of the cond.

- (do ((<*var*> {<*init*> {<*step*>}}) ...)
     (<*test*> <*expr*> ...)
     <*stmt*> ...)

  An iterative looping form, in which each <*var*> is initially bound to the corresponding <*init*> in an extended lexical environment. The <*test*> is then performed, and if true, each <*expr*> is evaluated, with the last returned as the value of do. If the <*test*> is false, each <*stmt*> is evaluated in sequence, each <*var*> is bound to the value of the corresponding <*step*>, and the <*test*> is performed again.

- (if <*test*> <*expr$_1$*> {<*expr$_2$*>})

  The <*test*> is evaluated, and if true, the value of <*expr$_1$*> is returned. If the <*test*> is false, the value of <*expr$_2$*> is returned if present, otherwise the value of the if form is unspecified.

A.3
LOCAL BINDINGS

- (let ((<*variable*> <*expr*>) ...) <*expression*> ...)

  The current lexical environment is extended to include the bindings of the <*variable*>s to the corresponding <*expr*>s in an undetermined order, and then the remaining <*expression*>s are evaluated in the extended environment, with the value of the last returned as the value of the let.

- (let* ((<*variable*> <*expr*>) ...) <*expression*> ...)

  Similar to let except that the <*variable*>s are bound in sequence.

- (letrec ((<*variable*> <*expr*>) ...) <*expression*> ...)

  Similar to let except that the <*variable*>s are also added to the extended environment, thus allowing for (mutual) recursion.

A.4
EQUALITY TESTS

(eq? *<obj> <obj>*)	Test for identical objects
(equal? *<obj> <obj>*)	Test for (structural) equivalence
(eqv? *<obj> <obj>*)	Test for string or numeric equivalence

A.5
LOGICAL EXPRESSIONS

(and *<expr> <expr>* ...)	Logical AND
(not *<obj>*)	Logical NOT
(or *<expr><expr>* ...)	Logical OR

Note that and and or are short-circuit evaluated. The sequential evaluation of the *<expr>*s ceases as soon as the final value is determined, e.g., (and #F (sqrt -3)) will return () with no error.

A.6
ARITHMETIC FUNCTIONS

(* *<num-expr> <num-expr>* ...)	Multiplication
(+ *<num-expr> <num-expr>* ...)	Addition
(- *<num-expr> <num-expr>* ...)	Subtraction
(/ *<num-expr> <num-expr>* ...)	Division
(= *<num-expr> <num-expr>*)	Test equality of numbers
(< *<num-expr> <num-expr>*)	Test numeric inequalities
(<= *<num-expr> <num-expr>*)	Test numeric inequalities
(> *<num-expr> <num-expr>*)	Test numeric inequalities
(>= *<num-expr> <num-expr>*)	Test numeric inequalities
(1+ *<num-expr>*)	Synonym for add1
(-1+ *<num-expr>*)	Synonym for sub1
(abs *<num-expr>*)	Absolute value
(add1 *<num-expr>*)	Add 1 to argument
(even? *<integer>*)	True if *<integer>* is even
(float *<num-expr>*)	Convert to floating point
(integer? *<obj>*)	True if *<obj>* is an integer
(max *<num-expr> <num-expr>*...)	Maximum of numbers
(min *<num-expr> <num-expr>*...)	Minimum of numbers
(minus *<num-expr>*)	Change sign of argument
(negative? *<num-expr>*)	True if *<num-expr>* is negative
(odd? *<integer>*)	True if *<integer>* is odd

(positive? *<num-expr>*)	True if *<num-expr>* is positive
(quotient *<int>* *<int>*)	Integer quotient
(remainder *<int>* *<int>*)	Remainder after integer division
(round *<num-expr>*)	Round to nearest integer
(sqrt *<num-expr>*)	Square root
(sub1 *<num-expr>*)	Subtract 1 from argument
(truncate *<num-expr>*)	Integer component of *<num-expr>*
(zero? *<num-expr>*)	Test for zero

A.7
RECOGNIZERS

(atom? *<obj>*)	True if *<obj>* is an atom
(boolean? *<obj>*)	True if *<obj>* is Boolean
(eof-object? *<obj>*)	True if *<obj>* is end-of-file marker
(float? *<obj>*)	True if *<obj>* is floating point
(null? *<obj>*)	True if *<obj>* is an empty list
(number? *<obj>*)	True if *<obj>* is a number
(pair? *<obj>*)	True if *<obj>* is a dotted pair
(string? *<obj>*)	True if *<obj>* is a string
(symbol? *<obj>*)	True if *<obj>* is a symbol

A.8
LISTS AND PAIRS

- (assoc *<obj>* *<list of lists>*)
  Return the first list in *<list of lists>* whose first element is equal? to *<obj>*.

- (assq *<obj>* *<list of lists>*)
  Same as assoc but test with eq?.

- (assv *<obj>* *<list of lists>*)
  Same as assoc but test with eqv?.

- (member *<obj>* *<list>*)
  Return tail of *<list>* beginning with first element that is equal? to *<obj>*.

- (memq *<obj>* *<list>*)
  Same as member but test with eq?.

- (memv *<obj>* *<list>*)
  Same as member but test with eqv?.

- (list-ref *<list>* *<n>*)
  Return the nth element of *<list>*, where n is a nonnegative integer, and the index of the first element of *<list>* is zero. Return the empty list if n is greater than or equal to the length of *<list>*.

`(append <list> <list>...)`	Append lists
`(car <pair>)`	Return first element of pair
`(cdr <pair>)`	Return second element of pair
`(cxxxxr <pair>)`	Combinations of `car` and `cdr`
`(cons <obj> <obj>)`	Make a pair
`(length <list>)`	Length of a list
`(list <obj> <obj> ...)`	Make a list of the `<obj>`s
`(reverse <list>)`	Return `<list>` in reverse order

A.9
STRINGS

`(string->symbol <str>)`	Create a symbol with `<str>` for name
`(string-append <str> <str>...)`	Append strings
`(string-length <str>)`	Return length of string
`(string-null? <str>)`	True if `<str>` is an empty string
`(string<? <str> <str>)`	Case sensitive comparison <
`(string<=? <str> <str>)`	Case sensitive comparison <=
`(string=? <str> <str>)`	Case sensitive comparison =
`(string>? <str> <str>)`	Case sensitive comparison >
`(string>=? <str> <str>)`	Case sensitive comparison >=
`(symbol->string <symbol>)`	Return string representing name of `<symbol>`

A.10
INPUT/OUTPUT

- `(call-with-input-file <filename> <proc>)`

  Evaluate `<proc>` (a procedure with one parameter) with its parameter bound to an input port, which is bound to the file whose name is `<filename>`.

- `(call-with-output-file <filename> <proc>)`

  Evaluate `<proc>` (a procedure with one parameter) with its parameter bound to an output port, which is bound to the file whose name is `<filename>`.

- `(with-input-from-file <filename> <thunk>)`

  Evaluate `<thunk>` (a procedure with no parameters) with standard input redirected to come from `<filename>`.

- `(with-output-to-file <filename> <thunk>)`

  Evaluate `<thunk>` (a procedure with no parameters) with standard output redirected to go to `<filename>`.

`(close-input-port <port>)`	Close an input file
`(close-output-port <port>)`	Close an output file
`(display <expr> {<port>})`	Write `<expr>` in human-readable form
`(file-exists? <filename>)`	Test for existence of file

(newline {<port>})	Write a carriage return
(open-extend-file <filename>)	Open a file for appending
(open-input-file <filename>)	Open a file for input
(open-output-file <filename>)	Open a file for output
(pp <expr> {<port> {<width>}})	Pretty-print <expr>
(print <expr> {<port>})	Write <expr> in machine-readable form, preceded by a carriage return and followed by a space
(read {<port>})	Read an <expr>
(read-line {<port>})	Read an entire line of text—return as a string
(write <expr> {<port>})	Write <expr> in machine-readable form
(writeln <expr> {<port>})	Write <expr> in human-readable form, followed by a carriage return

A.11
PROPERTY LISTS

(getprop <symbol> <property>)	Return the value corresponding to <property> on the property list of <symbol>
(proplist <sym>)	Return property list of <sym>
(putprop <sym> <val> <prop>)	Assign <prop> the value <val> in property list of <sym>
(remprop <sym> <prop>)	Remove <prop> and its value from property list of <sym>

A.12
DEBUGGING

(bkpt <message> <expr>)	Set a breakpoint
(trace <proc>)	Trace entries to procedure <proc>
(trace-both <proc>)	Trace both entries to and exits from procedure <proc>
(trace-entry <proc>)	Trace entries to procedure <proc>
(trace-exit <proc>)	Trace exits from procedure <proc>
(untrace <proc>)	Remove all tracing from <proc>
(untrace-entry <proc>)	Remove entry tracing from <proc>
(untrace-exit <proc>)	Remove exit tracing from <proc>

A.13
SCOOPS

- (compile-class <class>)

  Compile a SCOOPS class and install into proper place in object hierarchy.

- (define-class <name> {<attribute> <attribute> ...})

  Define a SCOOPS class.

- `(define-method (<class> <method-name>) (<param>..) <expr>..)`
  Define a method for handling a SCOOPS message.

- `(describe <SCOOPS class or object>)`
  Display information about argument.

- `(make-instance <class> {<var> <init> <var> <init> ...})`
  Return an instance of *<class>*, optionally with some instance variables initialized to given values.

- `(send <obj> <message-name> <argument> <argument> ...)`
  Send a message to a SCOOPS object.

A.14
MISCELLANEOUS PROCEDURES

`(apply <proc> (<arg> ..))`	Apply *<proc>* to arguments
`(edwin)`	Invoke the EDWIN editor
`(error <message> <expr>)`	Print error message and enter inspector
`(eval <expr> {<environment>})`	Evaluate an expression
`(exit)`	Exit SCHEME system
`(explode <obj>)`	Return list of one-character symbols from symbol name
`(for-each <proc> <list>)`	Apply *<proc>* to each element of *<list>*
`(implode <list>)`	Create a symbol whose name is made up of the first character of each element of *<list>*
`(load <filename>)`	Read and evaluate each of the SCHEME expressions in *<filename>*
`(map <proc> <list>)`	Apply *<proc>* to each element of *<list>* and return a list of the results
`(quote <obj>)`	Return *<obj>* unevaluated
`(set! <variable> <expr>)`	Assign *<variable>* the value of *<expr>* (*<variable>* must already be defined in some enclosing environment)
`(transcript-off)`	Turn off transcripting and close transcript file
`(transcript-on <filename>)`	Begin echoing all terminal interaction to *<filename>*

A.15
SPECIAL SYMBOLS

`PCS-DEBUG-MODE`	A variable that when set to #T allows full tracing and inspecting
`*THE-NON-PRINTING-OBJECT*`	A variable whose print name is not visible when displayed by the top-level `read-eval-print` loop
`#F`	Logical FALSE

NIL	Equivalent to #F
FALSE	A variable initially set to #F
#T	Logical TRUE
T	Equivalent to #T
TRUE	A variable initially set to #T

Some Handy Utilities

This appendix contains the SCHEME source code for the utilities used in the text. These are not necessarily examples of production-quality code, but are intended as simple functions/procedures that one can add to a PC SCHEME system to enhance the running of the examples in this text.

B.1
THE PROCEDURE demo

The procedure demo is used to execute a sequence of SCHEME expressions stored in a file and display the expressions and their values on the screen, as if the expressions were entered interactively at the top-level prompt. demo can be useful for demonstrating the action of a predefined sequence of operations, and for combining with the built-in SCHEME transcript facility to produce listings showing how a program executes.

```
(define (demo filename)
  (let ((demo-write
          (lambda (expr)
            (if (eq? expr *the-non-printing-object*)
                (display "")
                (write expr)))))
    (if (file-exists? filename)
        (with-input-from-file filename
          (lambda ()
            (newline)
            (display "===== Beginning of demo:  ")
            (display filename)
            (writeln " =====")
```

```
                (newline)
                (do ((expr (read) (read))
                     (n 1 (1+ n)))
                    ((eof-object? expr)
                     (newline)
                     (display "===== End of demo:  ")
                     (display filename)
                     (writeln " =====")
                     (newline))
                    (display "[D") (display n) (display "] ")
                    (write expr) (newline)
                    (demo-write (eval expr)) (newline))))
          (writeln "No such file."))
      *the-non-printing-object*))
```

The local function demo-write has been introduced, because write actually outputs *the-non-printing-object*, while in a demo we might prefer that nothing be printed. demo-write could probably be further enhanced to handle other special cases, such as writing 'x as 'x rather than the (quote x) that write writes. Such enhancements are left as an exercise.

B.2
THE PROCEDURE display-file

The procedure display-file introduced in Chapter 8 used recursion to loop through the entire input file. A more common way this might be programmed in SCHEME is to use the iterative looping form do, as shown here.

```
(define (display-file filename)
  (if (file-exists? filename)
      (with-input-from-file filename
        (lambda ()
          (newline)
          (display "===== Contents of ")
          (display filename)
          (writeln " =====")
          (newline)
          (do ((expr (read) (read)))
              ((eof-object? expr)
               (newline)
               (display "===== End of file:  ")
               (display filename)
               (writeln " =====")
               (newline))
              (pp expr)
              (newline))))
      (writeln "No such file."))
  *the-non-printing-object*)
```

Though pp was chosen as the print function for the expressions in the input file, one might want to try using write, print, display, or writeln for different output formats.

B.3
THE PROCEDURE display-text-file

The display-file procedure displays the SCHEME expressions in a file. A more general procedure might be the following, which simply echoes any text file to the screen.

```
(define (display-text-file filename)
  (with-input-from-file filename
    (lambda ()
      (do ((line-of-text (read-line) (read-line)))
          ((eof-object? line-of-text)
             *the-non-printing-object*)
          (writeln line-of-text)))))
```

B.4
THE PROCEDURE define-macro

Macros can be very useful, especially in developing a user interface to your programs, since they allow you to create special forms that do not evaluate their arguments. Unfortunately, the built-in macro syntax is somewhat less than obvious. The following macro allows you to define macros, using a syntax similar to the simplified define (no explicit lambda).

```
(macro define-macro
  (lambda (ee)
     `(macro ,(caadr ee)
        (lambda (e)
          (apply
            (lambda ,(cdadr ee) ,@(cddr ee))
            (cdr e)))))))
```

For example, we would define a macro lenq (which is just like the built-in length function, but does not evaluate its argument), as follows:

```
(define-macro (lenq l)
  `(length ',l))
```

(lenq (a b c)) would then return 3.

B.5
THE PROCEDURE load-if-present

Using define-macro, we can define a macro that loads a file only if it exists in the current directory, and that does not require you to put double quotes around the filename. If no file extension is given, ".s" is automatically appended to the filename.

```
(define-macro (load-if-present file)
  `(let ((filename
           (if (memq '|.| (explode ',file))
               (symbol->string ',file)
               (string-append (symbol->string ',file) ".S"))))
     (if (file-exists? filename)
         (load filename)
         (begin
           (display "File not found:   ")
           (display filename))))))
```

B.6
THE FILES PATCH.PCS AND SCHEME.INI

The files patch.pcs and scheme.ini are used to customize the initialization of your
SCHEME system. patch.pcs is normally located in your home SCHEME directory
and is used for patches that you want in effect whenever you use SCHEME. My
own version includes the definitions of the functions first, second, rest, etc., as well
as calls to load certain other utilities. For example, patch.pcs may contain:

```
(define first car)
(define second cadr)
(define third caddr)
(define fourth cadddr)
(define rest cdr)
(load "demo.s")
(load "disp-fil.s")
(load "def-mac.s")
(load "load-if.s")
```

On the other hand, scheme.ini is kept in the current working directory and should
contain initialization expressions to be evaluated only for this directory. We would
run different applications in different directories, each with its own scheme.ini. As
an example, scheme.ini might contain the following:

```
(set! pcs-debug-mode t)
(load-if-present myload)
(load-if-present mydemo)
```

where myload.s contains additional temporary initialization expressions and mydemo.s
contains a call to demo a particular file. Another (easy) exercise might be to define a
demo-if-present macro that works like load-if-present but appends ".DEM" if no file
extension is included in the argument.

Editing

So far we have been entering our PC SCHEME code directly into the top level of the interpreter. While this process is certainly quick and allows immediate results, it does not allow us any editing capabilities beyond backspacing along a single line. As our programs become more lengthy and complex, this will certainly prove inadequate, making an editor imperative. In this appendix, we discuss the editor supplied with PC SCHEME. Other SCHEME systems may have different editing systems.

C.1
LOADING ASCII FILES

We can actually use any ASCII text editor to write SCHEME code. After saving our work to a file (the standard SCHEME extension is .s), we can enter SCHEME and issue the procedure call (load *<filename>*), where the *<filename>* must be a string enclosed in quotes, e.g., (load "test.s"). The result of loading the file will be the same as if we had entered each of the pieces of code in the file directly into the SCHEME top level, but without having the returned values displayed.

It is possible to specify a full DOS pathname such as c:\programs\test.s in the load procedure, but you must realize that the backslash character (\) is used as an escape character in SCHEME strings. This means that in a SCHEME string, we must denote the backslash by a double backslash (\\). Thus, to load the file mentioned above, we would use (load "c:\\programs\\test.s").

As mentioned in Chapter 2, the files patch.pcs and scheme.ini are loaded automatically when SCHEME is invoked. Since these files are text files, they can be modified to include any valid SCHEME expressions, including additional calls to load. Using the SCHEME function file-exists?, we can even include conditional loading of files, such as:

```
(if (file-exists? "myload.s") (load "myload.s"))
```

which will check the current directory for a file named "myload.s" and try to load it only if the file exists. This would add one additional level to the patch.pcs/ scheme.ini hierarchy, allowing variations in initialization even for those directories that use copies of the same scheme.ini.

Simple calls to load can also be used in scheme.ini to allow the break-up of a potentially large file into several smaller files for ease of editing. Conceivably, scheme.ini could contain nothing but a sequence of calls to load. And, of course, load can be used interactively at SCHEME top level to add features on the run.

C.2
THE EDWIN EDITOR

PC SCHEME also provides its own text editor, EDWIN, which is based on the well-known EMACS editor, and is an adaptation of the original EDWIN editor developed at MIT. EDWIN is invoked by evaluating the parameterless procedure (edwin) in SCHEME. The EDWIN files are not normally loaded with the SCHEME system, but are automatically loaded when (edwin) is first evaluated. This means that the first time you call EDWIN in a given SCHEME session, there will be a delay while the system is loaded. Thereafter, EDWIN can be entered much more quickly.

Once EDWIN is loaded, the screen changes as you are put into the editor environment. Most of the screen is blank, awaiting text entry. The bottom two lines of the screen are the windows through which EDWIN communicates with the user. The first of these windows is the *mode window*, which is a single line in reverse video just above the bottom line of the screen. It includes the version number of EDWIN, the *mode* EDWIN is in (see the section on page 120, "Miscellaneous Commands"), and the file that is currently being edited, if any. The bottom line of the screen is in normal video and echoes the commands that you give and displays various editor messages and prompts.

EDWIN is a full-screen text editor with a few special features for handling SCHEME programs. Those with EMACS experience may find it quite familiar. (The file edwin.ini can be used to customize key assignments, but we will restrict our discussion here to the standard definitions for consistency.) EDWIN commands make use of a special "meta" key which is not found on PCs. As a substitute for the meta key, we can press the Escape key (ESC), or alternatively CTRL-Z, as a prefix before continuing with the rest of the command; e.g., a command listed as "meta-O" is entered by first pressing (and releasing) ESC and then pressing O.

Basic Cursor Control

The most basic cursor control is probably movement left or right one character and up or down one line. There are control key combinations for these cursor movements, but as an alternative, most people will use the cursor control keys on the keyboard, which work as usual. Some commands for movement over greater distances are given in the following:

Distance	Forward/Down	Backward/Up
One word	Meta-F	Meta-B
One screenful	CTRL-V	Meta-V
One expression	Meta-CTRL-F	Meta-CTRL-B

In addition, there are commands to move to the beginning or end of a given segment of the edit buffer:

Segment	To Beginning	To End
One line	CTRL-A	CTRL-E
One sentence	Meta-A	Meta-E
Entire buffer	Meta-<	Meta->

Cut and Paste Operations

EDWIN provides the ability to cut (or *kill*) sections of the edit buffer and paste (or *unkill*) them in new locations. There are several different kill commands, which can be found in Chapter 4 of the *PC SCHEME User's Guide* [SCHEME, 1987a]. For simplicity, we will look at only a few here. The most general command is to kill a particular selected, or marked, region. Of course, to do this, we must first be able to mark the region. This is done by positioning the cursor at one end of the region, setting a "mark" by pressing CTRL-@, and then moving the cursor to the other end of the region. The region can now be killed (cut and placed in a circular buffer called the *kill ring*) with CTRL-W or copied into the kill ring with meta-W. This text can then be unkilled at a new cursor location using CTRL-Y. Finally, a single line can be killed quickly using CTRL-K. To summarize:

Command	Keystrokes
Set a mark	CTRL-@
Cut a region to the kill ring	CTRL-W
Copy a region to the kill ring	Meta-W
Unkill	CTRL-Y
Kill a single line	CTRL-K

File Commands

EDWIN provides the usual commands for accessing files, such as loading, saving, and saving under a new name. In addition, one can write a marked region to a file and insert a second file into the current file at the cursor. Most EDWIN file commands require two keystrokes, the first being CTRL-X.

Command	Keystrokes
Load ("visit") a file	CTRL-X CTRL-V
Save the current file	CTRL-X CTRL-S
Write to a new filename	CTRL-X CTRL-W
Insert a file	CTRL-X CTRL-I
Write ("put") a region to a file	CTRL-X CTRL-P

Exiting EDWIN

Finally, EDWIN includes various commands for exiting the editor and returning to SCHEME. In addition to a simple return to SCHEME, we may evaluate a single expression, a marked region, or the entire buffer upon our return.

Command	Keystrokes
Exit EDWIN and return to SCHEME, leaving the edit buffer intact	CTRL-X CTRL-Z
Exit EDWIN and return to SCHEME, clearing the edit buffer	CTRL-X CTRL-C
Evaluate the entire edit buffer and return to SCHEME	Meta-O
Evaluate the next S-expression and return to SCHEME	Meta-CTRL-X
Evaluate the marked region and return to SCHEME	Meta-CTRL-Z

The evaluation commands require that EDWIN be in SCHEME mode as described below.

Miscellaneous Commands

EDWIN can operate in two modes, fundamental mode (for general text editing) and SCHEME mode. SCHEME mode is the default mode for the PC SCHEME system. In SCHEME mode, there are additional features that support SCHEME programming, such as parenthesis matching and automatic indenting of SCHEME expressions. Toggle between modes with CTRL-X CTRL-M.

Like other LISP dialects, SCHEME uses more than its share of parentheses. To aid the programmer entering SCHEME code, whenever a closing parenthesis, ")", is typed, EDWIN flashes the cursor on the matching opening parenthesis, "(". If the matching parenthesis is not currently visible on the screen, the first part of the expression is displayed at the bottom of the screen. EDWIN sounds a beep if there is no match.

Proper indenting can help one keep the structure of an expression clear to the reader. When entering SCHEME code, the next line is automatically indented properly if you press CTRL-ENTER instead of ENTER. Unindented lines of code can also be indented properly by placing the cursor on the line and pressing TAB. In addition to improving the appearance of your code, this automatic indenting can assist in discovering errors in the structure of your expressions due to misplaced parentheses, since these errors would result in unexpected indenting. Use of the indenting feature is highly recommended for these reasons.

Debugging Tools

D.1
TRACING

As our function definitions and the chains of function compositions get more complicated, we see that it would be helpful to follow the various calls and inspect their input and output. PC SCHEME provides just such a facility with a collection of tracing functions: trace, trace-entry, trace-exit, and trace-both. The purpose of these functions is to show us what values are passed to the parameters during a function call (trace, trace-entry) and what value is returned by the function (trace-exit). The function trace-both does just what you expect and traces both the values passed in and the value returned. As a demonstration, recall first the function sqr that we defined in Chapter 3. In the transcript below, we shall define, trace, and call sqr.

```
[1] (define (sqr x) (* x x))
SQR
[2] (trace-both sqr)
OK
[3] (sqr 4)
 >>> Entering #<PROCEDURE SQR>
  Argument 1: 4
 <<< Leaving #<PROCEDURE SQR> with value 16
  Argument 1: 4
16
[4] _
```

In order to remove tracing from a function, we call untrace, untrace-entry, or untrace-exit. (untrace untraces both entries and exits, in contrast to the tracing functions, where trace is equivalent to trace-entry rather than trace-both.)

```
[4] (untrace sqr)
OK
[5] (sqr 4)
16
[6] _
```

Of course, simple functions such as sqr are rarely a problem. Consider then the recursive function factorial, defined as:

```
(define (factorial n)
  (if (zero? n)
      1
      (* n (factorial (sub1 n)))))
```

Tracing this function before a call to (factorial 5) yields the following:

```
[1] (trace-both factorial)
OK
[2] (factorial 5)
 >>> Entering #<PROCEDURE FACTORIAL>
  Argument 1: 5
 >>> Entering #<PROCEDURE FACTORIAL>
  Argument 1: 4
 >>> Entering #<PROCEDURE FACTORIAL>
  Argument 1: 3
 >>> Entering #<PROCEDURE FACTORIAL>
  Argument 1: 2
 >>> Entering #<PROCEDURE FACTORIAL>
  Argument 1: 1
 >>> Entering #<PROCEDURE FACTORIAL>
  Argument 1: 0
 <<< Leaving #<PROCEDURE FACTORIAL> with value 1
  Argument 1: 0
 <<< Leaving #<PROCEDURE FACTORIAL> with value 1
  Argument 1: 1
 <<< Leaving #<PROCEDURE FACTORIAL> with value 2
  Argument 1: 2
 <<< Leaving #<PROCEDURE FACTORIAL> with value 6
  Argument 1: 3
 <<< Leaving #<PROCEDURE FACTORIAL> with value 24
  Argument 1: 4
 <<< Leaving #<PROCEDURE FACTORIAL> with value 120
  Argument 1: 5
120
[3]
```

It must be noted here that PC SCHEME compiles function definitions such as this and that the recursive structure is often lost. An attempt to trace factorial as above would, surprisingly, result in just the top-level call being traced unless we first (*before* defining factorial) reset the SCHEME system variable PCS-DEBUG-MODE to be true (#T). This is done with the set! command, which is described more fully in Chapter 9.

```
(set! pcs-debug-mode #T)
```

While learning SCHEME, and in general when developing programs, it might be advisable to include the above command in the initialization file scheme.ini so that such tracing and some other debugging techniques will always be available. Later this can be removed from scheme.ini to improve efficiency.

When tracing tail-recursive functions, we find that it is not necessary to trace the exits, since they will all be the same as the final value returned. In the following add function, we get all the information we need with a call to trace.

```
[3] (define (add x y)
      (if (zero? y)
          x
          (add (add1 x) (sub1 y))))
ADD
[4] (trace add)
OK
[5] (add 3 4)
 >>> Entering #<PROCEDURE ADD>
   Argument 1: 3
   Argument 2: 4
 >>> Entering #<PROCEDURE ADD>
   Argument 1: 4
   Argument 2: 3
 >>> Entering #<PROCEDURE ADD>
   Argument 1: 5
   Argument 2: 2
 >>> Entering #<PROCEDURE ADD>
   Argument 1: 6
   Argument 2: 1
 >>> Entering #<PROCEDURE ADD>
   Argument 1: 7
   Argument 2: 0
7
[6] _
```

We can trace more than one function at a time, though the output can get fairly cluttered if we are not careful. The following trace combines the above two functions with a new function, foo, which calls them both. Note that we can also combine various versions of trace.

```
[6] (define (foo x)
      (+ (factorial x) (add x x)))
FOO
[7] (trace foo)
OK
[8] (trace factorial)
OK
[9] (trace-both add)
OK
[10] (foo 4)
 >>> Entering #<PROCEDURE FOO>
   Argument 1: 4
```

```
>>> Entering #<PROCEDURE FACTORIAL>
 Argument 1: 4
>>> Entering #<PROCEDURE FACTORIAL>
 Argument 1: 3
>>> Entering #<PROCEDURE FACTORIAL>
 Argument 1: 2
>>> Entering #<PROCEDURE FACTORIAL>
 Argument 1: 1
>>> Entering #<PROCEDURE FACTORIAL>
 Argument 1: 0
<<< Leaving #<PROCEDURE FACTORIAL> with value 1
 Argument 1: 0
<<< Leaving #<PROCEDURE FACTORIAL> with value 1
 Argument 1: 1
<<< Leaving #<PROCEDURE FACTORIAL> with value 2
 Argument 1: 2
<<< Leaving #<PROCEDURE FACTORIAL> with value 6
 Argument 1: 3
<<< Leaving #<PROCEDURE FACTORIAL> with value 24
 Argument 1: 4
>>> Entering #<PROCEDURE ADD>
 Argument 1: 4
 Argument 2: 4
>>> Entering #<PROCEDURE ADD>
 Argument 1: 5
 Argument 2: 3
>>> Entering #<PROCEDURE ADD>
 Argument 1: 6
 Argument 2: 2
>>> Entering #<PROCEDURE ADD>
 Argument 1: 7
 Argument 2: 1
>>> Entering #<PROCEDURE ADD>
 Argument 1: 8
 Argument 2: 0
32
[11] _
```

D.2
PRETTY-PRINTING

When PCS-DEBUG-MODE is set to #T, the SCHEME code for functions is saved along with the compiled object code so that it may be retrieved and manipulated by other SCHEME functions, such as pp, the SCHEME "pretty-printer." Most of the time we will be entering our code using an editor such as EDWIN, allowing us access to the source code as we have entered it. However, there may be times when we define a function interactively at top level. Once such a definition has scrolled off the screen, we can no longer see what we keyed in. The pp function shows us the function definition, in a properly indented format, as shown on the following page, when applied to the function solve-quadratic-equation from Chapter 5:

```
[12] (define (solve-quadratic-equation a b discrim)
       (cond ((= discrim 0)
                 (find-one-solution a b))
              ((> discrim 0)
                 (find-two-solutions
                     (* 2 a) (- b) (sqrt discrim)))
              (else
                 '() )))
SOLVE-QUADRATIC-EQUATION
[13] (pp solve-quadratic-equation)
#<PROCEDURE SOLVE-QUADRATIC-EQUATION> =
(LAMBDA (A B DISCRIM)
  (COND ((= DISCRIM 0) (FIND-ONE-SOLUTION A B))
        ((> DISCRIM 0)
         (FIND-TWO-SOLUTIONS (* 2 A) (- B) (SQRT DISCRIM)))
        (ELSE '())))
[14] _
```

Pretty-printing can also be an effective debugging aid. Since pp acts on the actual function definition, and not on the programmer's intentions, unexpected indenting by pp can indicate misplaced parentheses in the originally typed code. As with automatic indenting in EDWIN's SCHEME mode, the computer can see what the eye may have missed.

The pretty-printing function pp is not limited to function definitions, but may be called with any SCHEME object as its argument. Indenting depends on the structure of the object. Additional optional arguments to pp allow printing to a file and a column width for the output. The general use of pp does not require PCS-DEBUG-MODE to be #T.

D.3
THE SCHEME INSPECTOR

In Chapter 1, we encountered the "Inspector" when we tried to evaluate (sqrt -5), and later when we attempted to evaluate undefined variables. At that time, we simply returned to top level by pressing [CTRL]-[Q]. Now we will take a look at some of our other options.

When an error occurs in the evaluation of a SCHEME expression, we enter the Inspector environment. Once inside the Inspector, the bindings in effect are those of the environment in which the error occurred. This will include bindings of actual arguments to function parameters, bindings introduced by the let form and its variations, and locally defined objects. We will be able to examine the various bindings, modify them if desired, and evaluate other expressions within the local environment, as well as to display a backtrace of the function calls that led to the current situation. A question mark (?) entered at the Inspector prompt causes a list of our options to be displayed on the screen.

The Inspector expects single-character commands, most of which are control-key combinations, such as the [CTRL]-[Q] command used for quitting. There are commands for inspecting the current environment bindings, such as on the following page.

CTRL-C	Display the bindings in the current environment
CTRL-V	Evaluate a single expression in the current environment (this command may also be activated by pressing the SPACEBAR)
CTRL-B	Display a backtrace of the procedure calls that led to the current breakpoint
CTRL-L	List the current procedure
CTRL-W	Display the currently active stack frame
CTRL-M	Display the breakpoint message that was originally displayed when the Inspector was invoked

We may also move to other environments, or to the stack frames of calling procedures, with the following commands:

CTRL-P	Move to the next outer enclosing (parent) environment
CTRL-S	Move back to the next inner (son) environment
CTRL-U	Move up to the stack frame of the procedure that called the current procedure
CTRL-D	Move back down to the stack frame of the procedure called by the current procedure

An exclamation point (!) reinitializes the Inspector.

Since we may evaluate expressions that may change bindings of local values and parameters, we can also resume the original evaluation with these new values, using:

CTRL-G	Resume the original evaluation from the breakpoint ("Go")

or we may quit using CTRL-Q, as mentioned previously.

User-Defined Breakpoints

Sometimes we may want to inspect the inner workings of a SCHEME procedure that does not have a run-time error. Perhaps the results are coming out wrong and we suspect a logical error in the procedure's design, or perhaps we just want to explore. We can do this by creating our own breakpoints in the procedure, with the SCHEME form bkpt, which takes two arguments, a string to be printed when the breakpoint is encountered, and an expression to be evaluated and returned. For example, we may wish to check the values of various parameters at some point during the solution of one of our quadratic equations, in which case we might modify the solve-quadratic-equation function as follows:

```
(define (solve-quadratic-equation a b discrim)
  (cond ((= discrim 0)
         (find-one-solution a b))
        ((> discrim 0)
         (bkpt "The discriminant is" discrim)  ;breakpoint
         (find-two-solutions
           (* 2 a) (- b) (sqrt discrim)))
        (else
          '() )))
```

We can then evaluate (solve 1 3 -2) and do some inspecting:

```
[1] (solve 1 3 -2)

[BKPT encountered!] The discriminant is
17

[Inspect] Current environment frame          ;Ctrl-C
Environment frame bindings at level 0
    A                       1
    B                       3
    DISCRIM                 17

[Inspect] Backtrace calls                     ;Ctrl-B
Stack frame for #<PROCEDURE SOLVE-QUADRATIC>
    A                       1
    B                       3
    DISCRIM                 17
  called from   #<PROCEDURE SOLVE>
  called from   ()
  called from   #<PROCEDURE EVAL>
  called from   #<PROCEDURE ==SCHEME-RESET==>

[Inspect] List Procedure                      ;Ctrl-L
#<PROCEDURE SOLVE-QUADRATIC> =
(LAMBDA (A B DISCRIM)
  (COND ((= DISCRIM 0) (FIND-ONE-SOLUTION A B))
        ((> DISCRIM 0)
         (BKPT "The discriminant is" DISCRIM)
         (FIND-TWO-SOLUTIONS (* 2 A) (- B) (SQRT DISCRIM)))
        (ELSE '())))

[Inspect] Up to caller                        ;Ctrl-U
Stack frame for #<PROCEDURE SOLVE>
    A                       1
    B                       3
    C                       -2

[Inspect] List Procedure                      ;Ctrl-L
#<PROCEDURE SOLVE> =
(LAMBDA (A B C)
  (PRINT-SOLUTIONS (SOLVE-EQUATION A B C)))

[Inspect] Go                                  ;Ctrl-G

The real solutions are:

    x = 0.56155281280883
    x = -3.56155281280883

[2] _
```

The Inspector can be a very important tool when constructing large SCHEME programs with many interacting procedures. As the complexity level rises, our ability to find bugs by staring at the source code, or even by tracing functions, diminishes. One of the things that has made the LISP family of languages popular over the years, in addition to its symbol-manipulation capabilities, is the rich interactive debugging environment provided.

References

Abelson, 1985   Abelson, H., Sussman, G. J., and Sussman, J. (1985). *Structure and interpretation of computer programs*. Cambridge, MA: MIT Press and McGraw-Hill.

Dybvig, 1987   Dybvig, R.K. (1987). *The SCHEME programming language*. Englewood Cliffs, NJ: Prentice-Hall.

Eisenberg, 1988   Eisenberg, M. (1988). *Programming in SCHEME*. Redwood City, CA: Scientific Press.

Pattis, 1981   Pattis, R.E. (1981). *Karel the robot: A gentle introduction to the art of programming*. New York: Wiley.

Scheme³, 1986   Revised³ report on the algorithmic language SCHEME. *ACM Sigplan Notices* 21 (12): 37–79.

Scheme, 1987a   *PC SCHEME: A simple, modern LISP: User's guide, revision B* (1987). Austin, TX: Texas Instruments.

Scheme, 1987b   *PC SCHEME tutorial* (1987). Austin, TX: Texas Instruments.

Scheme, 1987c   *TI SCHEME language reference manual, revision B* (1987). Austin, TX: Texas Instruments.

Scheme⁴, 1991   Revised⁴ report on the algorithmic language SCHEME. *ACM Sigplan LISP Pointers*, 4(3): 1–55.

Smith, 1988   Smith, J.D. (1988). *An introduction to SCHEME*. Englewood Cliffs, NJ: Prentice-Hall, Inc.

Springer, 1989   Springer, G., and Friedman, D.P. (1989). *SCHEME and the art of programming*. Cambridge, MA: MIT Press and McGraw-Hill.

Index